SAGGISTICA 3

Dennis Barone

America / Trattabili

Dennis Barone

America / Trattabili

Bordighera Press

Library of Congress Control Number: 2011907096

Cover art: Robert Dente, *Abandoned Sicilian Farm*, intaglio monoprint, 2007. Reproduced courtesy of the artist.

© 2011 by Dennis Barone

All rights reserved. Parts of this book may be reprinted only by written permission from the author, and may not be reproduced for publication in book, magazine, or electronic media of any kind, except in quotations for purposes of literary reviews by critics.

Printed in the United States.

Published by
BORDIGHERA PRESS
John D. Calandra Italian American Institute
25 West 43rd Street, 17th Floor
New York, NY 10036

SAGGISTICA 3
ISBN 978-1-59954-018-4

Acknowledgements

A number of chapters in this book have been published earlier in the following journals and magazines. They appear here in modified and updated form.

"Good Thing Great-Granddad Not 'Returned'." *The New Haven Register* July 18, 2007: A10;

"Study Hard: A Lesson Unlike So Many Others." *Voices in Italian Americana* 16.1 (2005): 19-34;

"Translating Identities: The Italian as Other in Two Early American Films." *Metro Magazine* 153 (2007): 173-177;

"Pascal D'Angelo and the Situation of the Italian American Writer." *Voices in Italian Americana* 13.2 (2002): 125-136;

"Immigrant Enigma: Pascal D'Angelo, *Son of Italy*." *Voices in Italian Americana* 11.2 (2000): 13-29;

"Anger and Assimilation in New York: Louis Forgione's *The River Between* (1928)." *Italian Americana* 22.2 (2004): 183-200;

"Rome If You Want To: The Currency of John Fante's Italy." *Forum Italicum* 37.2 (2003): 436-453;

"'Beating the Marbles Game': The Hagiography of John Fante." *Voices in Italian Americana* 15.2 (2004): 11-25;

"Pagano's Gold." *Italian Americana* 26.1 (2008): 71-82;

"'Machines Are Us': Joseph Papaleo and the Literature of Sprawl." *Forum Italicum* 42.1 (2008): 99-113;

"The Black Hand Becomes the Big Box: Two Poets of South Philadelphia–Resistance or Acquiescence?" *Italian Americana* 25.1 (2007): 37-47;

"'We've Always Been Different': Louisa Ermelino's Spring Street Trilogy and Italian American Women's Writing." *Critique* 48.1 (2006): 19-30.

TABLE OF CONTENTS

PREFACE: *Do Not Return to Sender* (1)

INTRODUCTION: *Epic or Eclogue* (8)

CHAPTER 1 • *The Italian as Other* (28)

CHAPTER 2 • *The Situation of the Italian American Writer* (38)

CHAPTER 3 • *Immigrant Enigma* (50)

CHAPTER 4 • *Anger and Assimilation in New York* (67)

CHAPTER 5 • *Rome, If You Want* (87)

CHAPTER 6 • *Beating the Marbles Game* (106)

CHAPTER 7 • *Pagano's Gold* (122)

CHAPTER 8 • *The Literature of Sprawl* (135)

CHAPTER 9 • *The Black Hand Becomes the Big Box* (152)

CHAPTER 10 • *Always Different* (163)

WORKS CITED (179)

INDEX (191)

Preface

Do Not Return to Sender

On February 17, 1942, the United States Department of Justice issued my great-grandfather, Alfredo Barone, an alien registration card. It included a photograph, a fingerprint, basic information such as color of the eyes and a warning to carry the card at all times. Failure to do so could result in "detention and internment."

Recently, in 2007, the Homeland Security Secretary Michael Chertoff defended immigration raids by Immigration and Customs Enforcement agents as part of Operation Return to Sender. One of the most remarked upon raids at this time occurred in New Haven, Connecticut. As I read about these raids, I thought of my great-grandfather, who in 1917 published his Italian Protestant evangelical newsletter at a house on Congress Avenue in the Elm City.

According to one policy expert commentator, New Haven's efforts to assist immigrants, including illegal immigrants, thwarted federal officials' ability "to remove potentially dangerous lawbreakers from the community." Again, I thought of my great-grandfather, who at five feet two inches and constantly quoting Scripture could not have been much of a national security threat.

But, what if he had been "returned to sender," as Immigration and Customs Enforcement so cleverly put it? In his proselytizing to Italian immigrants, he emphasized not only Bible-learning, but English lessons and Americanization skills. Indeed, the authors of a report published by the Italian Baptist Missionary Association in 1918 asserted "there can be no Americanization without evangelization." The belief such men held was that America is a Protestant country as well as an English-speaking one. This may be a narrow-minded, prejudicial view, but it hardly seems a threat to national security.

Alfredo's first son, Melchisedec, born in Foggia, Italy, in 1893, attended Columbia University and became a physician. My dad used to tell me that "Doc" never turned away a penniless patient during the long years of the Great Depression. Often, he received payment by way of a basket of figs or a bottle of homemade anisette.

My dad, Alfred, considered following in the footsteps of his father and pursuing a medical career. Two years into his undergraduate studies at New York University, he entered the service of his country—at just about the time his grandfather received an alien identification card. There was a real war going on then and yet America had room for a man who had no desire to ever become a U. S. citizen and for a man who would die, if necessary, for this country.

My dad served with honor and distinction. Indeed, when he died in April of 2006, we were moved, if not wide-eyed amazed, to see the number of medals and citations he had received. He was not one to brag. He never pursued the career in medicine, either. Like many young soldiers, he married during the war and when he returned from overseas he had a young family to support.

So, follow the narrative logic here. If my great-grandfather had been "returned to sender," there'd be no me! I have taught for more than twenty years at Saint Joseph College in West Hartford, Connecticut, an institution founded during the Depression that has an under-appreciated mission. Most of Saint Joseph's students are first-generation college attendees and many are the daughters of immigrants.

When Alfredo Barone received his alien identification card, he had been living in America for forty-three years. As a young man in Italy, he rejected the Catholicism of his prominent family and became a Protestant. Besides conversion to Protestantism and rejection of or by his family, he moved about a lot: his parental family resided in a small town near Naples, but Alfredo married on the other shore in Bari, his first son was born in Foggia and before leaving Italy in 1899 for America he listed Calitri as the place of residence for his growing young family.

Soon after he arrived here, he seemed to have as many addresses as Dunkin' Donuts would a century later: Monson and East Longmeadow, Massachusetts; several addresses in Stamford and New Haven, Connecticut; and several more in Brooklyn, New York. Along with has wife, Rosa, his place of burial is Woodland Cemetery in Stamford. The Barone family crest dominates their large funerary monument. I find this fascinating. Alfredo bought the plots and ordered the monument in 1925, after he had lived in the United States for a quarter century. He died in 1950, so he had twenty-five years to change his mind about the decoration. But though he left Italy in 1899, he never became a U.S. citizen nor changed his wish to have his final resting place marked with an Italian royal crest. Although he left a lot behind in the Old World, he also carried a lot over. I am glad the United States welcomed him and did not "return to sender."

One day a good friend and colleague of mine proposed at a divisional meeting that we use Humanities' funds toward a campus visit by novelist John Irving. He prefaced his proposal with the statement that Irving would be the first "major author" to visit the campus since Sherman Alexie came some years before. This got me thinking. I fully supported my colleague's proposal, but the prefatory comment perplexed me.

During my years at Saint Joseph College approximately one-hundred authors have come to the campus (some for repeat visits, too), almost all of them as my guests. Granted, many have been local writers or young writers or obscure ones, but also the list includes names like Denise Levertov and Paul Auster; Susan Howe and Robert Creeley. (Louise DeSalvo, Carole Maso, and Mary Caponegro have also read at SJC on my invitation.) If we use the Norton Anthology as test than neither Irving nor Auster would be major (they're not included), but Levertov, Creeley, and Howe as well as Alexie would be (they are included). Who cares? So, I thought that day. It's not (or shouldn't be) a competition (and if it is I guess Italian American authors are the real losers here).

I had no intention of combining the essays herein into book form. I told myself: concentrate on your own creative work. I told myself: if anyone wants to read these essays they can read them in *Critique, Forum Italicum, Italian Americana,* and *Voices in Italian Americana,* and so on. But sitting there that day in our Humanities Division meeting keeping score of major and minor, it struck me that I am *obliged* to attempt to pull this work together. Major and minor divisions be damned: these books, these writers are a pleasure to read—from Pascal D'Angelo to Louise DeSalvo, these authors and their writings deserve a wider audience and the growing body of scholarly work on Italian American literature is one way to foster that audience. It is an honor to add my voice, my understanding to this effort.

I realized that much of my work as a scholar has been geared toward the lesser known or obscure, giving some new attention—or even first time attention—if not a new life to a forgotten film about the film industry, *Stand-In* (1937), or to William Smith's 1760 lectures on rhetoric or to Emanuel Carnevali's poems of the 1920s. In the early 1990s I edited two half-issues of the *Review of Contemporary Fiction*: one on Toby Olson and one on Paul Auster. Has the former remained obscure and the latter become major?

Maria Laurino recalls that Governor Cuomo once asked her "were you always an Italian?" This is another important question, and a brilliant one, I think, and like Laurino I would stumble a bit in answering this question. Well, yes and no, I would say—to be honest. Well, what do I mean?

I grew up in suburban New Jersey. My mother's parents were Norwegian, but lived far away in California while my father's Italian parents lived nearby in Brooklyn. So our family did have identification with the Italian American experience, but, like Laurino's family in Short Hills, New Jersey, an experience filtered through a suburban blender and its Anglo-homogenizing effect. Also, my grandfather was a physician and so we did not directly experience the Italian American working-class tight knit urban village. For our family there was a river between us and ethnicity, a river we sometimes crossed on Sundays. Louis Forgione saw it reverse in the 1920s: in his novel *The River Between* ethnicity had its locus in New Jersey and on the other side of the Hudson were the bright lights of Broadway and other Anglo-American traps and temptations.

In 1991 at the Modern Language Association Convention in San Francisco, I organized a special session on and reading by Gilbert Sorrentino. I had conducted an interview with Sorrentino that appeared in the *Partisan Review* a decade earlier. In the interview we discussed literary innovation and Ezra Pound and William Carlos Williams. So, too, at the MLA panel the speakers focused on Sorrentino as experimental writer and not at all as ethnic-writer or even as ethnic-experimental-writer.

Were you always an Italian American? I can't remember if it occurred on my way to the special session or on my way to the reading, but in the elevator there in the San Francisco convention hotel I met Fred Gardaphé for the first time. He exuded friendliness and enthusiasm. He told me he looked forward to the session or the reading (as I say I can't recall precisely) by the great *Italian American* writer Gilbert Sorrentino. I believe I met his interest and enthusiasm with disbelief. It *literally* never occurred to me to conceive of Sorrentino as an Italian American. Indeed, I probably would have been more likely to look upon this James Joyce and Flan O'Brien influenced (but—yes—Brooklyn-raised) writer as Irish! I think there in that elevator I restrained, suppressed an arrogant laugh, but I also learned a lesson. It might have been then at that moment that I became Italian American.[1]

---

[1] The ethnic identity may be more secure, rather than less, in the next generation. Many of my nieces and nephews have traveled to Italy. My niece Nina, named after her great-grandmother, majored in Classical Studies at Emory and studied in Italy for a year. Since graduation, she has returned to Italy several times.

I sent some poems to *VIA*.² Then I started reading D'Angelo and Puzo, Forgione and Fante. I read deeply first and then I started to write about what I read. I also started to write poems and fiction both imaginative and out of memory focused very intentionally on Italian American experience. I think in the 1980s and early 1990s, identity had been either something in flux (hence the interest in and admiration for Paul Auster³) or something not to be trusted (hence my association with L=A=N=G=U=A=G=E Poetry). In the introduction to the 1994 anthology *The Art of Practice* I asserted what would become conventional wisdom of the time and the movement; that is, poetry should not be about an experience, but should be itself an experience. I thought that poetry rooted in identity and an experience prior to the act of composition would lead to a deadening and dull sameness. I still think this is a danger, though now I'd say it's not inevitable. But try this: take a copy of Barone and Ganick *The Art of Practice* and flip through the pages. Now take an identity or New Formalist anthology and flip the pages. What strikes the eye immediately is that in the latter two kinds of anthologies everything does look similar whereas our anthology has an immediately visible variety.

Perhaps, these essays herein on forgotten and lesser-known authors such as Pagano and Papaleo or ones little studied such as Ermelino and Barbarese are just another way to add variety to what might otherwise become dull and deadening repetition of what's already known: Hemingway, Hemingway, Hemingway—or what have you. At the end of the preface to *The Art of Practice* I repeated the word pleasure in the final sentence. Here, too, I'll say it has been a pleasure to become Italian American and it is indeed my pleasure to foster the appreciation for and understanding of this wonderful tradition of Italian American writing.

---

² See, *Walking Backwards*.

³ See my introduction, "Paul Auster and the Postmodern American Novel" in *Beyond the Red Notebook* (1-26).

America / Trattabili—America / negotiable: the chapters herein develop how Italian American authors of different times and generations negotiated this challenging terrain called America. From the immigrant pick and shovel poet Pascal D'Angelo sleeping in workers' camps and abandoned railroad cars and dreaming of an artist's life to the Colorado born John Fante trying to find a *juste milieu* between film and novel writing to Joseph Papaleo mapping his way in unending transit from city neighborhood to suburban street, all these authors; the words and characters in their writings weave complex identities situated between Italy and America; immigrant and native-born. The chapters that follow describe and interpret such on-going and unsettled negotiations.

Introduction

Epic or Eclogue

Even large rooms, if they are taller than they are wide, may seem confining and rigid. The tales, we are told, are tall, and the ocean, we know for a fact, is wide. The ship is in each syllable we speak. Ethnicity circumscribes and its inescapability is strange and marvelous. Soaked and run aground, each syllable may uncover its path to an imagined garden.

From San Francisco he sent figs home to Brooklyn, and he wanted to be sure that some reached his grandfather and grandmother. He had attained the rank of Technical Sergeant and Message Center Chief, responsible for a CDM 94 code device. When he made his last jump near Apari on the north tip of the northern island of the Philippines, he first pushed a motor scooter out of the plane and then he jumped. While other men had to walk, he got to ride the scooter, an advantage of rank. He had taken and passed the test for Aviation Cadet Training, but the day after he arrived at flight school in Colorado the government cancelled all pilot training. The war approached its conclusion and the demand for pilots had declined. After the war, he lived on Turk Street in San Francisco with his young family, and he worked for the railroad. He sent figs home to Brooklyn, to 208 Prospect Avenue. The even numbered side of this street no longer exists. Long ago it fell to highway construction, post-war change.

Before he entered the army, he attended New York University. He had hoped to follow his father into a professional career in medicine. He received several B- grades and, therefore, he believed that even if he had not been drafted, he would not have been able to enter medical school.

And so he would offer this advice to us daily, if not twice a day, "study hard," and that I did and that is—still—what I do: daily and all day long, too, or so, at times, it seems. And this is a suggestion for *how to study*.

❖

There is a form (formula) to history. There has to be a change—a before, during, and after—and an agent of change. If there is this form, is there also truth, or, at least, truth other than the form?

History is a tale told in the present about the past in order to perpetuate someone's power in the present.

(The proof lies in the pudding and the pudding lies in the bowl and the bowl lies in the kitchen and the kitchen lies in the house and the house lies in the town and the town lies in the state and the state lies in the country and the country lies in the world.)

What gets into the archive? At Mount Vernon the Distilled Spirits Council has rebuilt Washington's distillery so that we may see our father's entrepreneurial skill. The Distilled Spirits Council redefines the General and President to fit its interest. Two summers of archaeological work have gone into the project and yet the executive director of Historic Mount Vernon noted that it is now illegal to produce liquor for human consumption in an authentic eighteenth-century manner.

And a few years before this Pioneer electronics ran a series of advertisements that proclaimed: revolutionary! In one of the advertisements a modern day model in George Washington dress stands next to a television screen that shows the Washington Memorial. "Monumental Brilliance," the ad proclaims, "Pioneer's Revolutionary Projection Monitor." Another shows Paul Revere as depicted by Copley, but with a compact disc in hand instead of a silver bowl: "Not Evolutionary, Revolutionary," the copy reads in this instance of the campaign.

If you came from another planet that had been monitoring Earth radio signals or those signals sent out into the great void by the radio telescopes of the SETI Project and so you had some knowledge of Earth language systems and you landed safely and exited your ship and you looked down at your feet and found a penny and then walked a few steps more and then (behold!) you found a nickel, what would you do, what would you conclude? Might you not rush back aboard ship and signal the home planet that you've made a discovery: that as the Earthling's coinage increases in value the coin increases in size and therefore these must be a highly logical species.

You are excited. And you make your report and then you receive much praise from the highest commissioners. You return outside and proceed until you discover a dime. Now what do you do: make complicated revisions or simply look the other way. The promised promotion...

In 1921 John Horace Mariano reported that, "immigration to America [...] has proved that but few race characteristics, if any, are fixed" (210). In America, Mariano stated, the "skeptic" "will find what we call real characteristics almost obliterated from the faces of even the first generation. The sluggish Pole has become vivacious, the fiery Italian has had his blood cooled to a temperature approved by even the most fastidious of those who believe that fervor and enthusiasm are not signs of good breeding" (210).

Indeed, New York City had a sudden effect on the physical nature of the immigrant. According to Mariano, anthropologist Franz Boaz "found after measuring thousands of head forms that even in so short a period as one generation the long-headed Sicilian became round-headed in New York City while the round-headed Hebrew became longheaded" (224). And these changes in personality and physiognomy were most practical for "One of the results of the war [World War I] has been to develop a strong sentiment antagonistic to hyphenated citizenship" (205).

In 1948 physicist Leo Szilard published a short story about anthropologists from outer space who come to Earth, specifically to New York City. "Report on 'Grand Central Terminal'" describes the aliens' investigations. They choose as their first object of study, as the title suggests, New York's Grand Central Terminal—now deserted. Like good fieldworkers everywhere they depend upon direct observation. They find that cars are marked "either 'Smokers' or 'Nonsmokers,' clearly indicating some sort of segregation of passengers" (118). The aliens deduce that this segregation has to do with skin pigmentation. Other evidence confirms their analysis. Of course, for the reader, this interpretation, though very logical, is wrong. Szilard published this story again in his 1961 book *The Voice of the Dolphins*. To read the story in 1948 before Brown versus Board of Education of Topeka, Kansas is very different than to read it in 1961. And to read it in the early twenty-first century—when perhaps the irony might be lost entirely since all trains are "nonsmokers"—is very different again.

What did Szilard's aliens observe? Were their observations any good? Could they have attained accurate knowledge of the customs of the Terminal's former occupants as well as the artifacts—the cars—they had left behind? Is such knowledge possible? What happens to that alien with the penny, nickel, and dime when that alien comes across a quarter? *What happened when* is the question that history asks, but *what if* is the premise that narrative presupposes.

Once upon a time not too long ago in a place not too far away some people working in a common endeavor thought that perhaps they had an answer. If they did not precisely have an answer, they certainly did have a certain force, centralized by way of academic institutionalization. This was the strictly historicized approach to culture postulated by the American Studies department (known as American Civilization) at the University of Pennsylvania. All good things, though, must come to an end. On the University of Pennsylvania website under the link for American Civilization you can read the following: "the Department of American Civilization was officially ended by action of the University Trustees in March of 1994."

This is a story like many others. Let me use as my characters those paradigm dramas identified by Gene Wise in his brief history of American Studies published in 1979, and then add a few more to bring the tale to the present. These are: the intellectual-history synthesis, the myth-symbol school, societal relevance, the ethnographic method, poststructuralism-postmodernism-pluralism, and the imperial United States. The denouement of this narrative considers Cultural Studies and New Historicism and their relation to the above.

At the start of the American Studies movement in the 1920s scholars such as Vernon Louis Parrington believed that they could bring together what traditional disciplines take apart. Synthesis of sources and an ever-expanding range of possible sources has been a key feature of American Studies scholarship. While the early American Studies scholars sought a new synthesis, their conclusions were often elitist and unitary. As Wise points out, according to the intellectual history synthesis scholars, "There is an 'American mind.' That mind is more or less homogeneous" (306). Hence, the most well known book in this paradigm is Perry Miller's *The New England Mind* (1939). Gino Speranza, an Italian American, wrote in *The Atlantic Monthly* in 1920: "What *is* America, first and above all, if not the development, essentially, of Anglo-Saxon ways of thinking and doing, and more specifically, of New England ideas and ideals" ("Does Americanization Americanize" 267).

Even though Wise referred to a specific approach as a paradigm, the word does not fit in a strict Kuhnian way, for modes of American Studies scholarship continued to be practiced after their period of dominance and indeed continue in the present. Bruce Kuklick's work, for example, would exemplify the intellectual history approach in the present.

The myth-symbol school of the 1950s is the next paradigm that Wise identified. By this time in the 1950s American Studies has a secure institutional structure in the academy. There are programs at Harvard, Yale, Minnesota, Texas, and Penn. The American Studies Association began in 1949 and the *American Quarterly* in 1951. Various foundations and federal grants had helped fund American Studies programs and the Fulbright program disseminated the movement worldwide.

While one can fault the myth-symbol school for its tendency to essentialize, to argue that some myths and symbols dominate all America, one can praise it for expanding the range of sources beyond great books and into the popular and material. Trachtenberg wrote in 1982 (again, methods continue to be used and to be useful well beyond their hay day): "Figures of speech, tropes, images, metaphors: I take these as materials of prime historical interest [...]" (8). He used "incorporation" as an explanatory metaphor for late nineteenth-century events, but turned it here, there, and everywhere—for business, for literature, for politics. Cecelia Tichi in *Shifting Gears: Technology, Literature, Culture in Modernist America* said, "the pictorial quality of machines and structures *was easily* transferred into fiction and poetry" (my emphasis) and argued that "all these [Modernist American] writers freely developed symbolic meanings from pictorially vivid machines and structures, knowing that their readers were as familiar with these forms as they themselves were" (5). My guess is that what the Brooklyn Bridge meant to my grandfather is not the same as what it meant to Hart Crane. These two men may have viewed differently the same object. At any rate, the differences in vision were probably as important as the similarities.

In the decade of the 1960s the American Studies movement aimed for social relevance, but once again also broadened its scope. While the myth-symbol school used popular sources, it did so to establish a holistic and unitary culture. In the 1960s not only were popular culture, material culture, women's studies, and African American studies welcomed into American Studies programs and departments, but also the discipline moved away from the notion that there is a single holistic American culture.

In the 1970s the University of Pennsylvania, headquarters of the American Studies Association and the *American Quarterly*, fostered the ethnographic approach, the adaptation of anthropological methods to the study of America. At that time there was some discontent among scholars that studies were too broad and hence insignificant because of weak evidence and hasty generalization or else insignificant because of exhaustive particular research but no generalization.

How can we use the products of a culture to understand that culture? How can we learn the importance of the product of a culture to the society that produced it rather than its importance to us? If we only do the latter, have we accomplished anything or have we merely repeated what is already known? Is it possible to transcend one's frame of reference to understand some other frame? Is this attempt to do so, but itself a frame within a frame?

An anthropologist at the University of Pennsylvania, A. Irving Hallowell, who influenced scholars in the American Civilization department, believed that some concept of self is implicit in any work: be it a chair, a novel, or a shovel. He thought, too, that all cultures have some concept of self and he took this to be a universal, but cautioned that the attributes that define a self are various and vary in different times, different places. Furthermore, he stated that the concept of self, that self-image implicit in the work, could not be independent of that concept of self that is characteristic of the society in which the work was produced.

If two elements are in the same place and time they must relate and they cannot be independent. Therefore, the Am Civ department, as it was known, taught its students to find repeated and shared ideas, artifacts, customs, environments, and images in a culture localized in time and space. One can hear echoes of Spengler and Frobenius and Levi-Strauss in these lessons.

Culture the program defined as a learned system of language and behavior that has continuity beyond a single generation. As I sat in class in College Hall I thought of *2001* and how the ape near the start of the film finds other apes at its water hole and then gains an advantage when it discovers that an old bone can become a club, a weapon and we see a baby imitate the parent and then the film slows to slow motion and the arm with bone in hand goes up and down and up and down until it lets the bone free and it flies spinning into space where in a match cut it becomes a space station where Americans argue about a Soviet threat to moonscape territory.

This shared system that is geographically and temporally bounded shares with its members only a part. No one person can explain the totality of experience. Ben Franklin cannot tell us all about eighteenth-century Philadelphia. Daryl F. Zanuck cannot tell us all about twentieth-century Los Angeles. Mario Puzo cannot tell us all about New York.

Symbolic systems mediate experience and we are often unaware of the mediation. This shared system is shared regardless of class, age, sex, or occupation. It is that which is touched by all and that which all are touched-by. Does this approach have the danger of suggesting to the scholar spurious similarities?

In that classroom in College Hall we were told that culture rationalizes experience, that it makes experience meaningful. I thought of *Rebel Without a Cause*. When Jim and Buzz are about to engage in a deadly game of chicken, Jim asks Buzz why they do it and Buzz replies, "we have to do something." But this is experience outside the approved culture and this exploration on the outside, at least in this film, leads to death and destruction. Ah, I thought, that explains the name Plato. The ideal is ever confronted by the limitations of the real and so Plato dies in the course of the narrative. But certainly with the post-World War II entertainment industry we're talking about a civilization and not a culture.

And so our professor moved on to this term and defined it as a network of cultures. A civilization does not explain life: it maintains internal peace. Ah, I thought of the Federation and Captain Kirk. In order for internal peace to be maintained it is necessary for all participating cultures to sacrifice some of their ideals and become somewhat tolerant of all other cultures in the network. Civilization is chaos made suitable by compromise. And at this point I thought of Freud and *Civilization and Its Discontents*. All my thought did not and does not revolve around movies and television shows.

I thought that day of Emerson, for example: who said: "A Gothic cathedral affirms that it was done by us and not done by us. Surely it was by man, but we find it not in our man" ("History" 154). And so, he suggested, "we apply ourselves to the history of its production. We put ourselves into the place and state of the builder" ("History" 154). In other words, we must try to understand the work from the inside looking out rather than from the outside looking in. We already think we know where we stand. We must try not to impose some present-day and alien structure, criteria on the past.

In *The Madonna of 115 Street*, Robert Orsi says, "the symbols and gestures" of Italian Harlem "have meaning only in the entire religious world of Italian Harlem. We will see," he says, "from this perspective, that the Italian American attitude toward institutional Catholicism is explicable as other than sheer perversity: when church-going is approached as normative in itself or as indicative of a people's spiritual quality, then the people's own perceptions and values will be lost: but if we begin with the latter—with the people's perceptions, values, needs, and history—then we can better understand their religious practices and attitudes" (xviii). Orsi says near the end of his book: "Having set the festa in its proper place at the center of Italian Harlem, it becomes possible to understand popular theology critically, in the context of the total life of the community. Theology has a full context now; what is known of the whole life of the culture will inform and restrain what can be said about its theology" (220).

But how can the scholar know both the whole and the part and also the relation between? How can any scholar know the mind that saw as well as the artifact seen? What of, for example, the corruption of sources? A 2001 exhibit at the Yale University Art Gallery featured a work by Fra Angelico that had been cut into three pieces in the nineteenth-century. Clearly the work sliced in three was not the same object as it was in 1450, but restored and exhibited in the Louis Kahn designed Yale University Art Gallery instead of a church in Italy—was it then "restored" to the same object as in 1450? At a Yale seminar on religion and American history that same year I asked a speaker whose work was on Pentecostals, why if Pentecostalism was a rural mid-American movement did he write in his book mostly about Los Angeles and Chicago? He replied that urban Pentecostals published materials and so those printed sources that survive are urban even though the movement was rural. What goes in the archive? Remember, at Mount Vernon two years of archaeological work went into the reconstruction of the great entrepreneur's distillery, an authentic reproduction that nonetheless cannot produce liquor in an authentic manner. Ah, Bartleby. Ah, humanity.

Can we know a culture's world-view? New Historicists tell us that world-view is a myth imposed from the outside to perpetuate one's own interests. Is the ethnographic approach a newer version of myth-symbol, then? Is it predicated on the application of a false metaphor? In other words, does a culture separated from us in time differ from one separated from us in space? Is there a difference between immediate experience and a mediated experience? Is the possibility of a total view more likely across space than time? Have the powerful of the past decided—even for archaeological evidence—what remains in a way that the powerful of Bali or Rutgers *at this moment* cannot? Is this difference between ethnography across time as opposed to across space a difficulty to be overcome or is it a problem that challenges the whole notion of this kind of study?

The ethnographic approach to American Studies was part of the attempt to add a scientific dimension to the humanities that occurred in the 1970s. Poststructuralism and postmodernism and accompanying doubt that such an endeavor was possible supplanted aims for underlying truths. New Historicism in the 1980s attempted to restore a historical dimension to American literary studies and posited itself as opposed to both New Critical and Deconstructionist readings of texts. This idea of a historical dimension sounds a lot like American Studies. I sometimes think scholars (even those down the hall from one another) speak too infrequently to one another and that it was exceptional that Murphey and Garvan of the Am Civ Department at Penn spoke so productively with colleagues Hallowell and Wallace in the Anthropology Department at Penn. For example, despite a special issue on memory in 1989 of the journal *Representations* that included in translation an excerpt from Pierre Nora's work and despite the general interest of the American academic community in all things French, there was in the early 1990s little interest by American literary scholars in the discussions about memory that had proliferated in France and the rest of Europe. The fall 1995 issue of the American journal of literary scholarship *MELUS*, an issue devoted to "History and Memory," contains no reference to the extensive bibliography in this field. American historians, on the other hand, had been an active part of these discussions on memory. The historian Michael Kammen, for example, published *Mystic Chords of Memory: The Transformations of Tradition in American Culture* in 1991.

New Historicism brackets together literature, ethnography, art history, and other disciplines and sciences, and isn't this what American Studies does? The difference is an emphasis on power relations. Cultural Studies, too, has this emphasis on power relations. Whereas that older ethnographic American Studies method believed a scientific objective search for truth was possible, Cultural Studies is part of or parallel to the postmodern and poststructuralist doubt in the truth-seeking possibility of intellectual inquiry. New Historicism and Cultural Studies offer the addition of greater self-consciousness to a historical conception of culture.

In 1989 the United States Information Agency contributed almost 70% of the annual operating budget of the European Association for American Studies and now it contributes nothing. Perhaps, in a time when truth is no longer deemed necessary or relevant, scholarship is a luxury we no longer need. After the date of September 11, 2001 and the Iraq War of 2003 it is no longer deemed necessary to send as many Fulbright scholars around the globe or to invite as many scholars from other countries to the United States. We don't need to share ideas any longer, but rather, perhaps, to control thought and to offer only one single idea. And this is a narrative I think I've heard before. So quickly this nation shifted from slogans for diversity to slogans for unity.

Ramon Castellblanch noted in an op-ed essay that, "Latinos come from many countries with widely diverging histories and from some countries with many different regions. [...] We have been coming to the United States in migratory waves. [...] Some arrived last week; some many generations ago." He warned that projecting a unity of all Latinos rather than seeing diversity could promote racist attitudes. "It is shame," he said, "that U.S. news media leaders still see Latinos in one lump rather than as a mosaic of cultures and peoples."

There's an old adage about Italian immigrants: they didn't know they were Italian until after they arrived in New York. As the authors of the Federal Writers' Project study of *The Italians of New York* put it, "Paradoxical as it may sound, in many cases he [the immigrant] became an Italian proper only after a certain stay in the United States. [...] the dweller in the next village, was to him an 'alien'" (220-221). Before the Risorgimento, 1796-1870, and the unification and creation of the modern nation, separate states often under foreign rule divided Italy. For the South of Italy, the Mezzogiorno, unification meant little more than a different occupying army. Rule remained in a sense foreign for power resided in the North of the country. Whereas the North had all the industrial wealth, the South was almost entirely agricultural and agriculture faced numerous crises in the late nineteenth, early twentieth-century: drought, changes in the international market, so-called land reform that led to absentee landlords who owned huge tracts of land. The South also faced high levels of taxation. In the South taxes were believed to be usurious and exploitive and in the North any programs to aid development were characterized as waste because those in the South were believed to be illiterate and lazy. To taxation and starvation could be added the threat of conscription. Few wanted to be drafted to serve a government that seemed distant, uncaring, and exploitive as a foreign power. Conscription, taxation, failed land reform, and agricultural crisis combined with rapid increase in steamship transportation led thousands of men, and later families, to leave Italy for other European countries and North and South America. One-third of the population, mostly from the South, left the country during the years 1890-1920. Even as late as the mid-1940s, Italian intellectual Carlo Levi declared, "We can bridge the abyss [between Southern peasants and the Italian State] only when we succeed in creating a government in which the peasants feel they have some share" (250).

In *Monty Python and the Holy Grail,* King Richard proclaims that he is Richard! King of all the Britons! And a worker in a ditch asks: The Britons? Who are the Britons? Similarly the Southern immigrants in

New York in the early twentieth-century might have said, The Italians! Who are the Italians? Immigrants identified with the town or region from which they came and often settled on city blocks according to those designations. According to George J. Lankevich, by 1900 the census reported that New York "had 145,433 residents of Italian descent" and "by 1908 contained more than 500,000 Italians, more than the population of Rome itself" (123). Lastly, according to Lankevich, by 1950, Italians constituted "the single greatest ethnic component" in New York (188). Italian Americans remain the largest percentage ethnic group in New York City. Forty percent of the 9/11 victims at the World Trade Center were Americans of Italian heritage, but this is one fact of the national tragedy that one rarely hears. How does a community reveal itself to itself and to others and why?

Approximately fifty percent of those masses that arrived during the years 1890-1920 returned to Italy. Italian men wanted to send money home to Italy and to return to Italy. They wanted to improve their family's life in Italy, not start afresh in the Untied States. Stephen Steinberg has said that, "the real function of the liberal immigration policies of the period [...] was to flood the labor market in order to keep labor abundant and cheap" (38). Such immigration policy was not, he said, "a principled commitment to the idea of America as an asylum [...]" (11). These, too, are facts that it seems almost taboo to mention.

So, too, until recently, has been mention of the involvement of Italian immigrants in radical politics and labor movements. Lucio Ruotolo, retired English Professor at Stanford University and son of Italian American sculptor Onorio Ruotolo, said that his father's involvement in radical politics was completely unknown to him and he was "surprised to learn about *Il Fuoco*, the magazine he and Arturo Giovannitti created and co-edited in 1914, dedicated to 'radical change'" (1-2). Lucio Ruotolo recalls that his mother "would angrily interrupt her husband whenever he made an anti-capitalist statement in my presence" (2). His mother's intention, he says, was to make him "thoroughly American" (2). His father, too, after a point, "collaborated, often in print, in revising of their radical past" (2). What is the image a community reveals of itself to itself and others in order to perpetuate? Lucia and Onorio Ruotolo would remove the hyphen from their son's identity and render him strictly *American*.

America for the Southern Italians, Carlo Levi said, "is a land where a man goes to work, where he toils and sweats for his daily bread, where he lays aside a little money only at the cost of endless hardship and privation, where he can die and no one will remember him. At the same time, and with no contradiction in terms, it is an earthly paradise and the promised land" (123).

Using materials from a two-year oral history project completed at the City University of New York in 1970, Virginia Yans-McLaughlin concludes that whereas Jews had a sense of their own agency Italians felt manipulated by fate. The interviews recorded in the study reveal, she states, "the activism so commonly identified with the Jewish working class and the fatalism so often associated with Italian laborers and peasants" (273). Jewish immigrants saw "themselves as persons of worth, active in the center of their histories" (274), but "Italian speakers," she notes, "[...] characterized their past selves as relatively passive agents, unable to control their environment, not terribly interested in doing so" (277). In this analysis, a residual belief in *la forza del destino*, not the elimination of a hyphenated identity, is the central motivating factor for behavior.

Kathleen Conzen and David Gerber, et. al, have written that, "the invention of ethnicity sought to reconcile the duality of the 'foreignness' and the 'Americanness' which the immigrants and their children experienced in their everyday lives" (6). These authors entitled their essay "The Invention of Ethnicity," emphasizing that current theory does not postulate ethnicity as a fixed and natural category. One of America's most famous sociologists, Herbert J. Gan's thought that "ethnicity is largely a working class style" (196) and hence is thrown off with prosperity or else becomes a "symbolic ethnicity, an ethnicity of last resort [...]" (193). The children and grandchildren of rural, illiterate, unskilled immigrants, according to Richard Gambino, "since the 1960s have caught up with and surpassed the national average for formal schooling, as well as for income. Italian Americans are relatively recently arrived in the economic middle class and are increasingly successful in it" ("The Crisis of Italian American Identity" 282). Because of this success, have Italian Americans been absorbed and assimilated or is Italian American ethnic identification still strong, yet ever changing? As material life improved for Italian Americans, they seemed to have become more ethnic. Does a group want to feel ethnic when all that connects them to the past is gone, as some have suggested? Was the growth in Italian American ethnic identification in the 1960s and beyond a reaction to social change at that time, as others have suggested? According to Conzen and Gerber: "By 1960 [...] third and fourth generation Italian Americans unexpectedly began to assert their distinctiveness as part of a wider ethnic revival sweeping America. Italian Americans joined with other ethnics to renegotiate their ethnicities in the midst of a national political crisis [...]" (29). "What emerges as important" in this process of ethnic identity formation and reformation, they say, "is not how much of the 'traditional' culture has survived, but rather the changing use to which people put cultural symbols and rituals" (31). Maybe ethnicity is a working class style, maybe it's a middle-class luxury, and maybe it's a lot of things and not one simple single thing ever lasting and all encompassing.

Rudolph Vecoli said in an essay published in the late 1990s that "to be an Italian American today obviously means something very different from what it meant fifty or seventy-five years ago [...] that meaning varies according to geography, generation, gender, social class, and political disposition. We would be hard pressed to define what it is that we share as Italian Americans today, but of one thing I am certain: we are once again in the process of reinventing our ethnicity" (313). This book you hold in your hands or many others that you might also hold and the relatively new graduate program in Italian American Studies at Stony Brook, along with enlarging institutions such as the Calandra Institute of Queens College and the Italian American Museum and mass media expressions such as *The Sopranos* and *That's Life*, are part of the current negotiations.

While there were fourteen attendees at the Mark Twain session at the MLA Convention in New York in 2002 there were fifty at the Italian American Discussion Group session. While the Ezra Pound Society, an Allied Organization, has been suspended for not completing its necessary paperwork, which may be a sign of decreasing interest in the poet, the Italian American Discussion Group has one hundred and fifteen members and plans to apply to the organization for Division status. This shows the growing interest in the field and its institutionalization.

In a more than one hundred page manuscript entitled "These, Parents, Are Our Schools," early to mid-twentieth-century Italian American educator and novelist Garibaldi M. Lapolla said, "that education, taken in the sense of a pursuit of formal studies without intrinsic and ultimate utility, tho it still casts a spell over many people, is considered basically unnecessary or undesirable" and "formal education that results in the ability to engage in useful social tasks besides giving its possessor knowledge and other personal advantages is the more desirable type." Lapolla's sense of ethnic identity clearly differs from that of the one hundred and fifteen members of the MLA's Italian American Literature discussion group. Italian Americans can now be speculative as well as shoulder-to-the-wheel practical.

In his book *Italian Signs, American Streets*, the major book on Italian American literature, Fred L. Gardaphé divides Italian American narrative into three chronological categories: the poetic mode, "characterized by models of behavior based on divine models and a strong sense of destiny as the means of determining one's fate" (16); the mythic mode, characterized by "models of behavior based on heroic figures who inspire a struggle with destiny" (16); and the philosophic mode, characterized by "models of behavior based on humans as makers of their own destinies" (16-17).

I want to draw attention here to the repetition of the word destiny. One of the repeated and shared characteristics of Italian American literature is a struggle between the peasant Italian belief in fate and destiny versus an American individualism. The former emphasizes loyalty to the group and the latter, to the self. While the family may restrict individual growth, the market place may require an aggressiveness that would not be tolerated in the home. In Italian American literature one can see the self's conflict with America (Pascal D'Angelo), the self's conflict with its American self and Italian born parents (Mario Puzo), and grandparents who connect the self to a past out of which the protagonist forms an ethnic identity (Helen Barolini).

The immigrant group used writing to form new identities situated between an old rural folk culture and a new urban industrialized culture. This narrative form develops from first generation immigrants who hold on to their old ways, live in insular communities, and often made a half-hearted attempt to learn the language of their adopted land; to second generation men and women who are caught between one way of life at school and at work and another way of life at home; to members of a third generation who safely find, as Jerre Mangione put it, "sustenance, not embarrassment" from a now distant and receding past ("Finale" 308). While Italian American writers of earlier generations wrote directly about lived experience, authors of the present may write in response to that writing, to those stories and with knowledge of historical studies so that the writing by these authors can be stories about stories and this may be due as much to their place within a recently conceptualized tradition (think of Gay Talese's 1993 essay "Where Are the Italian-American Novelists") as it is to recent modes of meta-fiction.

The above statement points to readers and reading. We know that just as all prunes are plums but not all plums are prunes, so all writers are readers but not all readers are writers. In the 1996 "Preface" to the reissue of his second novel *The Fortunate Pilgrim*, Mario Puzo speculates that his novel "still holds its power, maybe more now than" thirty years ago. "The changes in the culture," he says, "and the change in women's roles, as well as the growing interest in ethnic subjects, have made this book in many ways contemporary" (xii-xiii). Emerson said, "A Gothic cathedral affirms that it was done by us and not done by us" and so, he said, "we put ourselves into the place and state of the builder" ("History" 154), but who is it that builds; who is that creator? If we are to "apply ourselves to the history of its production" (Emerson 154), then it is not *a* cathedral that should be our object, but *cathedrals*; not a material body, but a body of material localized in space and time. Puzo wrote *The Fortunate Pilgrim* in 1964 looking back at 1928 and the years that followed. How can we read it in the early twenty-first century without having in our thoughts that popular icon of the later twentieth-century, *The Godfather* (1969)? Puzo says that, "Whenever the Godfather opened his mouth, in my own mind I heard the voice of my mother" ("Preface" xii). The present day reader, however, hears the voice of the Godfather as he or she reads about Lucia Santa, the protagonist of *The Fortunate Pilgrim* that Puzo modeled after his mother. The contemporary reader might see Don Corleone as one part Lucia Santa and one part her son, Larry Angeluzzi, who knew "he would be powerful" and "felt himself, knew himself, as one destined for success and glory" (46).

Pietro di Donato told the same story four times. He wrote a short story (1937) called "Christ in Concrete" and then expanded this story into a novel (1939) also called *Christ in Concrete*. In 1949 he wrote the treatment for a film version and in 1960 he told the story one last time in a novel called *Three Circles of Light*. All of these autobiographical narratives tell the story of the tragic death in a construction accident of the author's father on Good Friday, 1923. The short story became the first chapter of the first novel version and so the father's death comes near the start and the remainder of the fiction tells of the aftermath and the role of the son (Paul/Pietro) in the family's subsequent struggles. The film and second novel versions, however, end with the death of Geremio, the father. And in the latter two Geremio is a womanizer and is far less heroic than in the earlier versions. In the film version Geremio betrays his fellow workers and along with the contractor Murdin hides work site safety violations. In the original story and in the earlier novel representatives of institutions—managers, priests, judges—are depicted in a negative manner and di Donato shows Geremio in solidarity with his fellow workers. A priest who offers no help in the first novel shows up at the end of the film to offer solace and guidance to the distraught widow and her family.

At Geremio's funeral as presented in *Three Circles of Light* an aunt criticizes Paul: "Wouldst Americanize yourself like "Jerry Philips"? Who lies in the box of the dead, here, "Jerry Philips" or Vastese Geremio di Alba? Buttock to buttock with the pasty, braying American savages would your father be, eh?'" (231). In *Christ in Concrete*, on the other hand, di Donato does much too create sympathy in the reader's mind for Geremio and antipathy for American society. The night before his death, we are told, "was a crowning point in the life of Geremio. He bought a house! Twenty years he had helped to mold the New World. And now he was to have a house of his own!" (6). Soon after Geremio's death a police officer remarks, "'oh yeah—the wop is under the wrappin' paper out in the courtyard!'" (26). Luigi tells his sister Anunziata, Paul's mother, "'The money that was to have bought your little house barely pays the burial and stone. You have no money'" (44).

Whereas in the later novel the individual receives blame for his problems in the earlier novel institutions are at fault. Geremio in the earlier novel says that he "'will convince'" Murdin "'that the work must not go on like this [...] just for the sake of a little more profit!'" (11). At a workmen's compensation hearing Murdin blames the accident not on safety violations but on the "'Eyetalian laborers'": "'The Eyetalians are good workers, when you watch them and take care of them like a wet nurse. But when not personally supervised they get themselves into all kinds of trouble. They're careless like children'" (132). Could it be that these versions *by themselves* and their differences *alone* can confuse actuality as much as Paul Revere and his CD or George Washington and his television?

We must enter the mind of the builder, Emerson says. But I would suggest "we put ourselves into the place and state of" (Emerson, "History" 154) builders, not one single builder. Always pluralize: builders and buildings. Then we can use the products of a culture to understand a culture. We can learn the importance of the product of a culture to the society that produced it rather than its importance to us. Forget the promulgation of Great Art for it is naught but a tautology: great art has been esteemed through the centuries and it has been esteemed through the centuries because it is great art or great art tells us more of its time and it tells us more of its time because it's great art. Through observation and analysis of the repeated and shared localized in space and time it is possible to articulate patterns which connect so that meaningful cultural *hypotheses* may be formulated and supported. To do so is not to quit at the wake of master narratives and shake with doubt; nor is careful analysis the enemy of ethnic pride. No, to do so is just to exercise some cautious steps in the midst of a paradigm drama. Follow these steps, if you will, in the pages that proceed.

CHAPTER 1

THE ITALIAN AS OTHER

In his essay "The Mafia and The Movies: Why is Italian American Synonymous with Organized Crime?" Ben Lawton says that in the nineteen-teens "the identity of Italian Americans and crime in America had not yet been established" and that the idea would not take hold until the 1930s (80). In the early decades of the twentieth century, however, there were many examples of films that already depicted Italians as the prime example of what eugenicist Madison Grant referred to in his 1916 book *The Passing of the Great Race* as one of the "lower races" (5). The negative depiction of Italians in film may have even established an important pre-condition for the passage on anti-immigration legislation in the subsequent decades.

In the Mary Pickford vehicle *Poor Little Peppina* (1916), for example, Italians are associated with crime and threatening sexuality. In *The Italian* (1915), a film that on first viewing may seem a sympathetic depiction, Beppo Donnetti (George Beban) is represented as the stereotypical Italian immigrant as pejoratively described by Jacob Riis: "gay, lighthearted and, if his fur is not stoked the wrong way, inoffensive as a child" (*How the Other Half Lives* 45). Furthermore, both films employ a plot conceit that robs the immigrant a voice by allowing a sly cultural usurpation to take place. Beban, an actor who specialized in portraying melodramatic and tragic Italian immigrants, frames the story by appearing as his "real" self and reading a book called *The Italian*. Beban then falls asleep and dreams that he has become the key character Beppo Donnetti. At the tale's conclusion, Beban wakes up and realizes he only dreamed of being an Italian. Similarly, at *Poor Little Peppina*'s conclusion we discover that Pickford's Peppina is not an Italian after all, but the lost child of wealthy Anglo New Yorkers. The message in both films is clear: the foreign other must be wholly absorbed or else destroyed. There can be no co-existence, no pluralism.

Richard H. Brodhead has identified "two images of Italy in late nineteenth-century America": tourism to Italy and "mass migration from Italy to the United States [...]" (1). He refers to the latter image as the "alien-intruder Italy" and he notes that "the Italian immigrants of the late nineteenth century were largely read through this generalized image of the foreigner as agent of contemporary instability [...]" (5). The mind of one person, according to Brodhead, could indeed hold the strangely divergent views of Italy as apotheosis of the Grand Tour and as the homeland of barbarian invaders overtaking American soil.

The Italian and *Poor Little Peppina* exemplify these contradictory views. In the former, Beppo is a jovial gondolier in Venice who becomes a murderous barbarian in New York, and at the start of *Poor Little Peppina* we see a rich American family residing in a palatial Italian villa—until the Mafia strikes.

Richard Gambino claims the following: "Influenced by post-war Italian movies, Americans see Italian sexuality either as frank and earthy or as wanton in the fashion of *la dolce vita*" (*Blood of My Blood* 183). But the image of the Italian as barbarian was established during the Gilded Age, the years of film's birth, as well as by nineteenth-century literature such as Henry James's *Daisy Miller* (1878). If the Italian as sexual barbarian has a long history in American culture, so, too, does the Mafia image. These images are not only evident after the gangster films of the 1930s. For example, Christian McLeod's 1908 *The Heart of the Stranger: A Story of Little Italy* and Louis Forgione's *Men of Silence* of 1928 are novels that capitalized on the scandal of Italian and Italian-American crime—the cultural groundwork, in other words, for the stereotypical image of Italian-Americans in popular culture had been well established before the "talkies" gave us the harsh sounds of gunfire.

One film scholar who has argued for a silent-era origin for the sexual-Mafioso image of Italian-Americans is Giorgio Bertellini. Italian immigrants, he writes, shaped their sense of Italian national identity through the Italian films they saw ("Italian Imageries" 32). Native New Yorkers, on the other hand, shaped their sense of Italian immigrants through the American-made films that depicted Italians and Italian Americans ("New York City and the Representation of Italian Americans in the Cinema"). Both representations skewed reality. Bertellini believes that "criminality, 'Mafia,' or a general state of illegality—have been constant narrative patterns" of Italian-American characters in American films from the very start of the industry ("New York City" 116). Such depiction, he asserts, must be seen as part of "the history of Italians' classification with the USA's racial consciousness: a dynamic simultaneously subterranean and public, which preceded and accompanied the aesthetic patternings of Italian-Americans in American cinema" (116).

Part of the ideological project of such "aesthetic patternings," according to Bertellini, is to keep the immigrant "unassimilated" (116). Although he says that the image crystallized in the 1930s (after having provided a sizable list of relevant films from before that decade), he concludes: "In brief, American cinema's depiction of Italians as darker, more impulsive, and violent was from the very beginning engaged in racializing subjects perceived as threatening the social and economic stability of the New York civilized, that is 'White,' community" ("New York City" 117).

What Bertellini asserts runs counter to a well-established belief about American cinema. American films are supposed to endorse a melting-pot mentality, one in which difference is obscured by a shared sense of community. Lester D. Friedman, for instance, in his introductory essay for *Unspeakable Images: Ethnicity and the American Cinema* speaks of "total assimilation" and claims that ethnic characters "strive to melt silently into American society rather than to maintain any deep sense of ethnic identity" (26). Yet, in *The Italian* and *Poor Little Peppina* we see immigrants maintain their separateness; we see this separateness depicted as a threat and not as strength; we see that those who could not melt had to be eliminated. For Italian-Americans this "Americanness" is not so much "bland" (Friedman's word) as it is prejudicial and malicious.

At the same time that the American film industry sought to expand its audience base from primarily working-class to middle-class, the sought-after and more affluent audience was steeping itself in theories of degeneration and eugenics. Madison Grant's influential *The Passing of the Great Race* (1916) exemplifies such ideas and beliefs. He argued that not only could former slaves and current immigrants not be assimilated, but that what such groups contributed to the national profile would alter it in a profoundly dangerous and destructive way:

> It has taken us fifty years to learn that speaking English, wearing good clothes, and going to school and to church, does not transform a Negro into a white man. Nor was a Syrian or Egyptian freedman transformed into a Roman by wearing a toga, and applauding his favorite gladiator in the amphitheatre. We shall have a similar experience with the Polish Jew, whose dwarf stature, peculiar mentality, and ruthless concentration on self-interest are being engrafted upon the stock of the nation. (14)

Grant asserted that "the Slovak, the Italian, the Syrian, and the Jew" in combination had begun to "exterminate" the native-born American race (80-81). Therefore, he advocated "segregation or sterilization" (47) before New York produced "many amazing racial hybrids and some ethnic horrors that will be beyond the powers of future anthropologists to unravel" (81).

In *The Italian*, Beban's Beppo is represented as being sweet and childish in an Italian setting. In the USA, he is at first unassimilated, then violent. At the end of *The Italian*, a death in the main narrative and the framing device conspire to eliminate the character entirely. In his recent book *Hollywood Italians*, Peter Bondanella wonders at the wisdom of employing "such a strange parenthesis to enclose the narrative" of *The Italian* and concludes that "one obvious explanation is to convey that Beban is a legitimate theatrical performer" (24). This appears to me to be a weak conjecture.

Beban played many film roles and specialized in Italian characters. Born in 1873 in San Francisco, his film career included work as a writer, producer, director, and editor as well as an actor. His career ended prematurely in 1928 when he died as a result of a horseback riding injury. As a film actor, he played lead Italian characters in many films. Furthermore, he does not appear to have looked down on film, as Bondanella's words imply. In fact, Beban often attempted to bridge film production and stage performance. In New York he combined these artistic genres in work he wrote, directed, and performed. For instance, a film of his began and at some point the image on the screen came to life on the stage. The story continued and concluded in that live-action form. He did this, for example, in *The Loves of Ricardo* (1926), a dual-genre melodrama about an immigrant grocer.

If not an attempt "to convey that Beban is a legitimate theatrical performer" (Bondanella 24), what then is the explanation for the framing device? It seems to me that the film is an attempt to keep America from what Madison Grant called "a racial abyss" (228). Beppo is, indeed "the Italian." As the poet Vachel Lindsay wrote in the year of the film's release, Beppo "represents in a fashion the adventures of the whole Italian race coming to America [...]" (70). Rhetorically speaking, the film portrays the death of Italy through the death of Beppo's son Tony. Hence, the great race remains pure and uncontaminated. Beppo's line ends, his child dies; there is no Italian-American offspring—no hyphenated identity to disrupt the native-born.

The Italian stays well within the confines of Grant's "great race." The actor Beban subdues and subsumes the alien Beppo, and Beppo's new-world child dies. The closer Beppo moves to Beban's world, the more threatening he becomes. It Italy, Beppo was a picturesque prankster, smiling and innocent. In lower Manhattan he is a politician's pawn and would-be murderer. By simply crossing an ocean, the singing gondolier transforms into "an urban savage" and "a socially dangerous outsider," to use Bertellini's phrases for the image of the Italian-American male in film ("New York City" 117). This image of Beppo or the Italian as alienated and violent is further "crystallized" in the 1930s gangster films.

The death of Beppo's son Tony is a significant indicator in the narrative. In Venice, Beppo has a competitor for Annette's hand (Clara Williams). Annette's father gives Beppo one year to attain sufficient income to provide a stable home for his daughter or else she will wed another. Beppo sets off for America, "the Golden Land," as an intertitle calls it. In New York, slum boss Big Bill Corrigan offers Beppo money for his aid in securing the Italian vote for the Corrigan flunky. Beppo unquestioningly accepts the money. He brings Annette to New York, they marry, and a year later they have a son. A heat wave smothers the city. Their son Tony becomes ill. Two thugs rob Beppo of his meager savings. Beppo gradually becomes enraged and attacks them with a wrench. A policeman arrives and Beppo, not the thieves, gets dragged away. Corrigan appears. Beppo breaks free of the policeman's grasp and begs Corrigan for help. But Corrigan rejects Beppo and kicks him off the running board of his moving automobile. While Beppo sits in a jail, little Tony dies and Annette does not know what has happened to her husband. Released, Beppo returns home.

A month later, Beppo discovers that Corrigan's child has been struck with a serious illness and hovers near death. Beppo plots his revenge. Disguised as a peddler, he will enter the Corrigan residence and smother the child. In the child's room he sees that the child not only sleeps exactly like his own son did, but even makes a similar gesture. Beppo can't go through with the crime. We then see Beppo tending Tony's grave. Fade out. Fade in and Beban reads the last page of "The Italian," a curtain closes on the actor, and, thus, ends the movie of *The Italian*.

Beppo's child and Corrigan's child, linked by an innocent gesture in sleep, could have formed a new hybrid identity, except for the irrevocable fact that little Tony is dead. But the death of immigrant children made a lot more sense to Madison Grant than their "preservation." "Efforts to indiscriminately preserve babies among the lower classes," he wrote, "often result in serious injury to the race" (44). As Grant further puts it, "The laws of nature require the obliteration of the unfit, and human life is valuable only when it is of use to the community or race" (45). In the Darwinian wilds of lower Manhattan, Tony had been proven unfit, and despite the cuteness of his gesture when asleep, he could not have made a significant contribution to the community for the simple and irrefutable reason that he did not and could not belong to the "great race."

The Mary Pickford vehicle *Poor Little Peppina* has a kidnapping, an escape, cross-gender disguises and a coda that reasserts the cultural status quo. In this film of shifting identities, an American child residing with her wealthy parents in Italy becomes the victim of a Mafia kidnapping and is brought up as a poor Southern Italian teen. She fights off her cruel suitor and escapes to America disguised as an Italian boy. After various adventures, authorities in New York first discover that she/he is a girl and then that she is the long-lost, and believed to be deceased, only child of wealthy New Yorkers. She then becomes betrothed to a wealthy and gentle New York Assistant District Attorney. The Italians in the film are almost all evil members of the Mafia, except for Peppina's brother in her adopted Italian family.

The film opens with an intertitle: "Robert Torrens, a wealthy American, residing in Italy with his wife and only daughter, Lois." Then an iris shot opens to reveal a happy and close father, mother, and daughter. Alas, their bliss will be short-lived for there are problems with the house staff. Franzoli Soldo (Antonio Maiori), a Mafia boss now disguised as a butler working for the Torrens, drinks too much. Another member of the staff informs his employer of the repeated indiscretions. Torrens fires Soldo. We then see the Torrens family pray together. Soldo then kills the informer. Torrens gives chase and Soldo literally jumps into the arms of two passing *carabineri*. Soldo gets his day in court. Villato (Cesare Gravina), another Mafia member, is at the trial. Soldo gets convicted and sentenced, but Villato and colleagues spring him from prison. It is time for more revenge. Soldo and accomplices kidnap Lois. The kidnappers make it appear that a man (Soldo) and a child (Lois) have drowned. The Torrens give up all hope. Soldo, meanwhile, takes Lois to his relatives Dominica and Bianca (N. Cervi and Mrs. A. Maiori respectively) and their son Beppo (Jack Pickford, Mary's real life brother). Soldo tells them to raise the child as theirs—or else. Soldo goes to America.

Years pass. Lois, unaware of her American parentage, grows up. Her name is now Peppina. An American heiress known as the duchess has taken an interest in her, and teaches her English. To escape the advances of a cruel *padrone*, Peppina asks the Duchess for help. The Duchess provides her young protégé with money and her brother's calling card. At the engagement feast Peppina rejects her suitor and runs away. While changing into Beppo's clothes she loses the card of her New York contact. Beppo cuts Peppina's hair—a big moment for Pickford fans. Disguised as a boy she sets off for America.

She/he boards a ship in Naples as a stowaway. By chance, Hugh Carroll (Eugene O'Brien), the Duchess' brother, happens to be on the same ship. Overcome with hunger and still dressed as a boy, Peppina sneaks into a first class cabin to steal some food. It is Hugh's cabin and he catches her, but he is kind and he gives her a plate of food and then pays for her fare in steerage.

Meanwhile Soldo and Villato now own an East Side bar. They have decided to send for "Lois" to reunite her—fifteen years after the kidnapping—with her parents in New York. They believe this action will enable them to collect a large reward from the grateful parents. Peppina, in an effort not to burden Hugh, decides to go ashore with the ship's stoker. As chance would have it, he takes her/him to Soldo and Villato's. Unaware of her true identity, they trick Peppina into letting them hold her money for safekeeping. They take it and then put poor little Peppina to work for them. They are cruel to her. They even use her to try out their counterfeit money for them. Hugh tries to find out what happened to the boy on the ship. At the same time, the use of counterfeit money comes to his attention and we find out that he is an assistant District Attorney for the City of New York.

Peppina sneaks away from the bar and is eventually arrested. "Under cross-examination," an intertitle states, "Peppina has confessed that she is a girl." Hugh enters the room and once more helps. Police raid the East Side bar and capture Soldo and Villato. Peppina explains how and why she left Italy disguised as a boy. Due to a letter Beppo wrote to Soldo and Villato explaining that "Lois" could not be returned to her rightful parents because she ran away, Villato confesses and the authorities discover Peppina's truest identity: not only is she a girl but, as an intertitle exclaims, "Why, Chief! That's the Torrens child!" Lois is reunited with her parents. Three years pass. Hugh and Lois are to be married. The social order has been restored and all Italians have been rounded up and removed from the narrative. There has been no assimilation.

In *Our Movie Made Children*, a summary of social science research undertaken in the late twenties regarding film's impact on youth, Henry James Forman stated that some immigrant groups cannot be assimilated and that Italians are an especially troublesome group. Movies are persuasive, he asserts at the start of his book:

> "A movie a week" is with us a national slogan, almost a physical trait absorbed by the children with their mother's milk. Can we doubt that the influence of the motion pictures must of necessity bulk large in our national life, in the lives of our children, when it is practically universal? (16)

He saves one of his most powerful arguments for his penultimate chapter, his final substantive one before a brief summary. Here he speaks of "a congested area of New York City" and the Italians who "predominantly" live there (252). This neighborhood, he says, "is neither a League of Nations nor a melting pot" (252). It is a place of "murder, kidnapping, organized violence, hold-ups, burglary, racketeering and bootlegging [...]" (252).

And yet in this neighborhood, like so many others, "the great and established source of entertainment is the motion picture and the movie theatre" (253). Unfortunately, according to Forman, in such a troubled area "gangland pictures draw the greatest number of young people"

(254). This is especially pernicious for young boys who spend more time at the movies than anywhere else other than school and home (256). These boys "growing up in homes in which old-world patterns of life still dominate feel they are becoming Americanized and picking up American ways by means of the motion picture" (257).

Forman then considers the effect of one particular film *Little Caesar* (Mervyn LeRoy, 1931). In an area, he states, where children are "in actual contact with the underworld" such films have disastrous results. He describes the crimes of three "'Little Caesar' sequels": two are Italian American boys and one is Jewish American. Through a combination of bad movies and bad origins, Forman believes, the children of immigrants grow into bad men.

Horace Kallen, known as the founder of cultural pluralism in America, desired an accommodation of cultural differences in a democratic society. In his 1924 book *Culture and Democracy in the United States* he proclaimed that "the cultural prospect has been enriched, not depleted by the immigration, settlement, and self-maintenance in communities of peoples of all Europe upon the North American continent" (231). Furthermore, he believed, that "democracy involves, not the elimination of differences, but the perfection and conservation of differences" (61). Kallen helped found the New School for Social Research in New York City, but the West Coast institution known as Hollywood heard the voices of separatism more than those of pluralism.

If *The Italian* and *Poor Little Peppina* have significance as examples of early American film immigration narratives, then what the industry advocated was not "the perfection and conservation of differences," but their silencing and removal from cultural discourse. What the industry promoted even at this early stage in its history was not an innocent and "bland conception of Americanness" (Friedman 24), but a prejudicial and malicious one.

CHAPTER 2

THE SITUATION OF THE ITALIAN AMERICAN WRITER

In January 1925 *The New York Times Book Review* author chosen to write on Pascal D'Angelo's extraordinary immigrant autobiography, *Son of Italy*, gave it a mixed review. The reviewer said that the book has "a candor that is disarming, even if a bit affected." The half-hearted praise begins at the very start of the review: "'Son of Italy,' 'the pick-and-shovel poet': these titles plumb both the strength and weakness of one of the few Americanized immigrants whose success has been non-worldly yet decisive." The reviewer offers Edward Bok and Jacob Riis as two immigrant figures who typify "the practical, solid achievement that constitutes mundane success," whereas D'Angelo's "success is so spiritual as to be almost entirely devoid of material embellishments." It is indeed unusual in the genre of immigrant autobiography for the individual concerned to seek artistic success rather than material comfort. The claim by the *Times* reviewer that D'Angelo's success was spiritual rather than material contradicts the earlier claim that D'Angelo became "Americanized." D'Angelo's sort of success did not fit the standard American pattern. Perhaps because he did not become "Americanized," D'Angelo's autobiography had some modest audience reception in 1924, but except for an Arno Press reprint in 1975, it had not been republished until Guernica Editions of Toronto reissued it in 2003.[1] On the other

---

[1] In 2000 Jim Murphy published a book for adolescents entitled *Pick & Shovel Poet: The Journeys of Pascal D'Angelo*. This condensation of D'Angelo's story published prior to the republication of the actual work seems a sort of injustice to me. It is as if D'Angelo has been denied his own voice; his story wrenched from him and used (perhaps even trivialized) by another. Murphy frames extensive quotations in words that recontextualize the original in an inaccurate way. In doing this, he sugarcoats D'Angelo's harsh criticism of America. For the best previous writing on *Son of Italy* see Boelhower and Gardaphé. The Guernica edition of *Son of Italy* does not include Carl

hand, Bok's and Riis's autobiographies went through many printings and Bok's won a Pulitzer Prize. D'Angelo didn't "Americanize" and a comparison between D'Angelo and Bok and Riis reveals not only a vast difference between them but shows the Northern European taking center stage while the Southern European remained off stage and relegated to the margins of American life.

I take my title from an essay by Isaac Rosenfeld, "The Situation of the Jewish Writer," that he first published in the *Contemporary Jewish Record* in 1944. In this brief, cogent essay Rosenfeld claimed that "the position of Jewish writers—artists and intellectuals in general—is not entirely an unfortunate one. For the most part the young Jewish writers of today are the children of immigrants, and as such—not completely integrated in society and yet not wholly foreign to it—they enjoy a critical advantage over the life that surrounds them" (122). The advantage, according to Rosenfeld, can be stated quite simply: "Jews are marginal men" (122). Near the end of the essay he said, "Today nearly all sensibility—thought, creation, perception—is in exile, alienated from the society in which it barely managed to stay alive" (123). D'Angelo was not Jewish, but nonetheless there is a great affinity between what Rosenfeld said about Jewish American authors and this Italian American one. Whereas D'Angelo's experience is very different from Bok's and Riis's, it is in significant ways very similar to the Jewish American authors that Rosenfeld wrote about. Pascal D'Angelo's autobiography and his life after its publication reveal the experience of a marginal man, not an assimilated American.

Even the titles of the autobiographies of Bok and Riis differ from D'Angelo's. Riis titled his autobiography *The Making of an American*, not *Son of Denmark*. Bok titled his autobiography *The Americanization of Edward Bok*, not *Son of the Netherlands*. During the harshest moments of his struggle to stay one step ahead of starvation while working prodi-

---

Van Doren's introduction. Antonio D'Alfonso, publisher of Guernica Editions, told me, "The introduction was valid back then. Not now. I always find it condescending" (e-mail message, 24 September 2003).

giously on his poems, D'Angelo says, "I had learned the great lesson of America: I had learned to have faith in the future" (171). Nonetheless, he titled his autobiography *Son of Italy*, not *The Americanization of Pascal D'Angelo*. He remains loyal to his old-world group even as he asserts his new-found individualism. Carl Van Doren says in his introduction to *Son of Italy* that D'Angelo's "fame might have enabled its possessor to accept any one of several editorial positions, but he had the artistic tact to decline them all. After paying so high a price to be a poet, he was not willing to take his reward in some meaner coin" (xi). D'Angelo's decision to reject this "meaner coin" had a political origin as much as if not more than an aesthetic one. As D'Angelo wrote in his letter to Van Doren, which comprises five of the book's last six pages:

> I am not deserting the legions of toil to refuge myself in the literary world. No! No! I only want to express the wrath of their mistreatment. No! I seek no refuge! I am a worker, a pick and shovel man—what I want is an outlet to express what I can say beside work. Yes to express all the sorrows of those who cower under the crushing yoke of an unjust doom. (181)

This outlet he found in his published poetry in which he expresses these sorrows. For example, one poem entitled "The Toilers," printed in *The Literary Digest*, 14 October 1922, begins:

> Brown faces of immatured senility
> Twisted into an ecstasy of unshaped satiation.
> Eyes that are huge, tumultuous flares of light
> Peering athwart the forced austerity of tiredness.

And moving from a description of despair to an exclamation of bitterness, the poem ends:

> Your thoughts!
> Amid the incessant whirrs of the maniac motors,
> Are smashed into fragments of an irresolved
>   dream,
> And you are swept on! On!

By the involuntary rapids of meniality,
In frenzied whirls of humiliation.
On! On!

Pascal D'Angelo remained on the margins of American society in order to tell of the agonies of immigrants. Riis and Bok entered the mainstream of American society and although Riis fought for better living conditions for the urban poor, like Bok, he fought for his individual material success.

One of the facts that make Riis's and Bok's life stories very different from D'Angelo's is that the former two came from very different backgrounds than D'Angelo. Both Riis and Bok were from Northern European middle-class and highly literate families. D'Angelo came from the large landless Southern Italian peasant class. His parents were illiterate and, despite being from the region of Ovid, he did not grow up in a culture of books. Historians, journalists, and politicians often talk about north versus south dichotomies, whether within a single country such as Italy, for the entire European continent, or for the planet as a whole. Even today in the Netherlands residents of the wealthy northern Randstad region refer to the poor southern province, Limburg, as "Limbabwe." The year D'Angelo's autobiography was published, 1924, saw the enactment of restrictive immigration legislation that closed the door to America for southern and eastern Europeans.

A report published by the Italian Baptist Missionary Association in 1918 claimed that "A Man may live for 25 years in America, learn English, live 'a l'Americana' and yet be unfit for naturalization. On the other hand, a man may come from an English speaking country, or any other country, and stay in America 25 days, but intellectually, morally and spiritually he is well qualified to become an American citizen at once" (15). The authors of this report noted, "When the Pilgrim fathers established themselves here, their aims, endeavors and purposes were centered toward one direction: To found this Country on the immovable principles of Christianity, according to the teachings of the Scriptures. It was this fact which has made America the greatest, strongest, wealthiest and most distinguished nation of the world" (19). To be fully Americanized, the authors believed, means to be Protestant and hence they asserted, "there is no Americanization without Evangelization" (20). In this regard, too, Riis and Bok had an advantage over D'Angelo. Furthermore, in order to perfect his art, D'Angelo assumed characteristics usually associated with Eastern European Jewish immigrants, not those characteristics associated with Anglo-Protestant life.

Riis's father was the senior master in the Latin School in the town of Ribe, Denmark. Although the family's finances were stretched to their limits because of its large size, Riis states, "Of the whole fourteen but one lived to realize his hopes of a professional career, only to die when he had just graduated from medical school" (*Making of an America* 22). When he journeyed with his father to America, D'Angelo left behind in Italy, penniless, his mother and a younger brother. When Riis was a boy in Ribe his family knew the King of Denmark and at the end of his autobiography Riis recalls, "I saw him often when I was a young lad" (426). D'Angleo, on the other hand, saw the sheep he herded. Like D'Angelo, although he had to struggle mightily when he came to America, Riis had "a strong belief that in a free country [...] things would come right in the end [...]" (*Making of an American* 35). Yet in describing his early struggles at various jobs such as coal mining there is something cavalier in Riis's expression. The agony of manual labor described in D'Angelo's writing does not appear in Riis's. In addition to hope for a better future, Riis, like D'Angelo, aspired to be a writer. In this respect what *The New York Times Book Review* author said in the review of *Son of Italy* is somewhat unfair: for Riis didn't simply calculate how best to achieve material security. He sincerely wanted to be the best police news reporter in New York City and this aspiration led to his well-known work as a social reformer. Yet, writing police news reports is very different and much more practical for getting on in American life than writing poems about workers' struggles.

Early in his narrative, Riis notes that he came to America with letters of introduction "to the Danish Consul and to the President of the

American Banknote Company, Mr. Goodall" (*Making of an American* 39). He never used these letters, but the fact that he had them illustrates how very different Riis's immigrant experience was from D'Angelo's who came without any letters, in every sense. I am reminded of my own life experience and that of my grandfather's. I came from a very secure middle-class home. Yet, during graduate school my wife and I lived in a pitiful hovel. We knew another graduate student who lived in a beautiful, contemporary apartment high above Rittenhouse Square. Now I would never say that we were poor or that our experience could be in anyway compared to that of the urban poor of America. We were graduate students at the University of Pennsylvania and no matter how awful our dump we still shared much more with our fellow student high above elegant Rittenhouse Square than with the Philadelphians residing in run down post-war municipal housing. Similarly, my grandfather was born in Foggia in 1893 and immigrated with his parents and two sisters in 1899. As I noted in the "Preface," his father was part of the Italian Baptist Missionary movement, and he was a very literate man, the author of two books on theology and many pamphlets and newsletters. D'Angelo was sixteen when he came to America in 1910. Again, comparison here would be of apples and oranges. It is an amazing story that my grandfather attended the Monson Academy and Columbia University from which he received his medical degree in 1918, but it is so different from D'Angleo's story. My grandfather no doubt worked very hard at Columbia, but he worked at Columbia, not building state roads in Suffern, New York, as D'Angelo did.

Most often, Riis, like D'Angelo, blames much of the cause for urban poverty in America on the American economic system, not on a weakness in individual citizens or individual immigrant cultures. At one point in his autobiography Riis exclaims, "Only tramps [...] that was what we had made of them with our infernal machinery of rum-shop, tenement, dive [...]" (262). Riis believed that "Human nature is at bottom good, not bad" (*Making of an American* 293) and he had a strong dislike for people who "were of the school which professes to believe that everything proceeds from the love of self" (*Making of an American* 361), but he also believed that this innate goodness needs a spark to fire it and this is why he so admired Theodore Roosevelt.

> Good land! what are we that we should think ourselves always right, or, lest we do wrong, sit idle all our lives waiting for light? The light comes as we work toward it. Roosevelt was right when he said that the only one who never makes mistakes is the one who never does anything. Preserve us from him; from the man who eternally wants to hold the scales even and so never gets done weighing—never hands anything over the counter. Take him away and put red blood into his veins. And let the rest of us go ahead and make our mistakes—as few as we can, as many as we must; only let us go ahead. (*Making of an American* 325)

Riis wanted to strike a balance between doing well in America and doing "good" in America, but such a benevolent balance was not a possibility for D'Angelo. D'Angelo's concerns had nothing to do with either doing well or doing good, but everything to do with survival.

Riis makes the statement that "a little starvation once in a while even is not out of the way. We eat too much anyhow, and when you have fought your way through a tight place, you are the better for it" (*Making of an American* 300). It would have been impossible for D'Angelo to say such a thing. Indeed, in *Son of Italy* he recalls that "we would be so tired that with the pot still boiling on the two stones and the steam pouring up we would probably be half asleep and many a man has lost his supper because the fire galloped along freely while he nodded. And finally when the smoke and bad odor awoke him the supper is hopelessly burned in a dirty pot. And many a time, tired and mad, a man has gone to sleep without eating" (129).

Riis tended to offer a systemic explanation for urban poverty in America, not to blame particular immigrant cultures or individual members of a cultural group. Yet according to Riis in *How the Other Half Lives*, the problems of Italian immigrants are partly their own fault. Although the Italian is "gay" and "inoffensive as a child," "He not only knows no word of English, but he does not know enough to learn.

Rarely only can he write his own language. Unlike the German, who begins learning English the day he lands as a matter of duty, or the Polish Jew, who takes it up as soon as he is able as an investment, the Italian learns slowly, if at all" (42). Bok, on the other hand, blames the individual immigrant entirely for any lack of success in America. America, according to Bok, is, but for a few shortcomings that he lists at the end of his autobiography, a wonderful country and proof of this wonder, he asserts, is that "a little Dutch boy unceremoniously set down in America unable to make himself understood or even to know what persons were saying [...] was destined to write, for a period of years, to the largest body of readers ever addressed by an American editor [...]" (viii). Bok's autobiography was a bestseller and Pulitzer Prize winner. Perhaps, in 1920 at the height of Americanization efforts this autobiography by the long time editor of *The Ladies' Home Journal* spoke to the American reading public in a way that D'Angelo's book in 1924 at the height of immigration restriction could not speak.

Again, like Riis, but unlike D'Angelo, Bok came from a well to do and very literate family. Bok's father had made, however, "unwise investments" (1) and so the family—as a whole—came to America when young Bok was seven. Although he left school at thirteen, he notes that he had "the national linguistic gift inherent in the Dutch" and therefore "the English language was not so difficult of conquest" (4). His father drilled him in English every night. Pascal and his father slept exhausted on wooden slats in shanties every night.

Bok's father died when he was eighteen. Bok and his brother at this time "determined to have but one goal: to put their mother back to that life of comfort to which she had been brought up and was formerly accustomed" (61). (Bok wrote most of his autobiography in the third person.) At this goal, the two ingenious Dutch boys succeed. In fact, Bok can't understand why others don't succeed in attaining their material aspirations in this grand country. He writes in a chapter entitled "The Chances of Success": "he found every avenue leading to success wide open and certainly not overpeopled" (119). In fact, "He looked at the top, and instead of finding it overcrowded, he was surprised at the few who had reached there; the top fairly begged for more to climb its heights" (120). Whether or not one made it to the top, according to Bok, "was up to the man" (157).

In America, Bok concludes, "a man can go as far as his abilities will carry him" (448), for "no limitations are set except those within himself" (449). Those who do not succeed, according to Bok, probably did not learn the lesson of thrift. Indeed, "what was thrown away in a week's time from Brooklyn homes would feed the poor of the Netherlands" (435). This, according to Bok, is one of America's great faults. "There was literally nothing in American life to teach me thrift or economy; everything to teach me to spend and to waste" (435).

D'Angelo learned different lessons. Waste was not an issue for him because he had nothing to spend and so nothing to save. The commissary system in the United States made sure of that. As D'Angelo writes, "In its most extreme workings it results in perpetual peonage of the unlucky laborers who get caught" (110-111). He adds, "If you try to save money and spend very little [at the company store] you will find when pay day comes that you are charged with as much debt as someone who ate his fill" (112). Indeed, "the man who does not spend enough usually gets fired after a few warnings" and "a man who drinks every cent he earns is considered a 'good' man" (112).

In the first of a series of essays on Americanization that Bok commissioned for *The Ladies' Home Journal* in 1919, Esther Everett Lape claimed, "There is surely nothing dangerously un-America in spaghetti" (35). In this first essay, "Putting America Into Your City," Lape emphasized how important it is for immigrants to belong to American organizations because through their membership and, more importantly, their participation they will learn American values. She asked, "Do the foreign-born *belong* to the community sings of your city, your community kitchens, art associations, trade unions, women's clubs, chambers of commerce, civic committees?" (35). D'Angelo's mother, like most mothers of Mezzogiorno boys who immigrated to America, remained in Italy awaiting the return of her son. Immigrants, like D'Angelo and his father, "are migratory," according to Lape, "simply because they never find any city or community that offers them any inducement to settle down" (36). If only the D'Angelos' West Virginia work camp had offered them a "community sing" instead of a usurious camp store!

Spaghetti may not have been "dangerously un-American" in the early twentieth-century, but American leaders saw all hyphenated identities as a threat to national unity. In a speech delivered in October 1915, former President Theodore Roosevelt said, "There is no room in this country for hyphenated Americans. [...] There is no such thing as a hyphenated American who is a good American" (qtd. in Gambino *Blood of My Blood* 118). Immigrants had to be Americanized, homogenized. Frances A. Kellor in a *Yale Review* essay of 1919 entitled "What Is Americanization?" defined the term as "the science of racial relations in America, dealing with assimilation and amalgamation of diverse races in equity into an integral part of its national life" (285). The immigrant, Kellor claimed, must understand American ideals. "The native-born American," she said, "is the keeper of these ideals" (299). One might wonder how much "equity" there could be if only the native born are the "keepers" of that which Kellor claimed to be most essential.

"Only a brave man can be a brave artist, let alone a good one, in a hostile world," Rosenfeld said in "The Situation of the Jewish Writer" (122). D'Angelo, indeed, was brave. In a world of Americanization movements and restrictive immigration legislation he told some very harsh truths about Bok's land of endless opportunity. D'Angelo, as Rosenfeld said of the Jewish writer, had to be a marginal man in order to witness and to tell of this cruel reality.

As we saw in the "Introduction," many writers on the American immigrant experience have described commonalities and differences between Jewish and Italian immigrants. Jerre Mangione, for example, has noted that the two groups arrived at the same time, lived in the same neighborhoods, belonged to the same unions, and "placed great emphasis on the sanctity of the family" ("A Double Life" 177). The Italian immigrants, however, Mangione has observed, were mostly rural peasants not urban merchants ("A Double Life" 177-178). Because of the peasant background, the Italians were among the most illiterate of all immigrant groups. According to Stephen Steinberg, fifty-four percent of southern Italian immigrants were illiterate whereas only twenty-six percent of Eastern European Jews were illiterate (102). Steinberg has concluded that "one would not expect an urban proletariat [Jews] to exhibit the same values as peasants [Italians] emerging from folk societies and semi-feudal conditions" (103).

One of the differences in values often cited is that while Jewish immigrants desired an advanced education Italians were anti-bookish and anti-intellectual. At most, it is often said, Italian immigrants favored only a practical, career-training education. Gay Talese recalls in his [in]famous essay "Where Are the Italian American Novelists?" that there were no books in his house or in his Italian American friends' houses when he grew up. Talese says that his teachers tried to force him into the technical school track because, his teachers believed, Italian Americans by nature didn't go to college. A younger Italian American author, Marianna De Marco Torgovnick, says that she had to fight to enroll in college preparatory courses for everyone assumed that an Italian girl from Bensonhurst would be a secretary. In the preface to *Crossing Ocean Parkway* she writes, "For me, upward mobility was a two-step process: first, identifying with school, and hence with Jewish culture rather than the Italian American group into which I was born; then, moving into universities and middle-and upper-middle class America" (vii). Similarly, the first major Italian American novelist, Pietro di Donato, became close friends with a young Jewish intellectual, Louis Ducoff, and in his autobiographical novel, *Christ in Concrete*, di Donato describes the importance of this friendship.[2]

In many ways it is useful to see Pascal D'Angelo as similar to the Jewish American writer that Rosenfeld described. As he becomes inter-

---

[2] See my memoir-essay "Cairns" for more about the relationship between Pietro di Donato and Louis Ducoff.

ested in language and poetry, D'Angelo, already marginalized from the mainstream, becomes also marginalized from the margin. He becomes in someway an outsider from his own immigrant group. D'Angelo says that when he started writing he "became the cause of considerable argument among" his "fellow-workers" (158). They argued whether or not knowledge of English would do an Italian immigrant laborer any good in this hard world. One old worker beaten down by years of physical toil advises D'Angelo, "'You should get a job in some office where you can use your English and you can learn more'" (159), but D'Angelo can think only of something as impractical as his poetry: "I dreamed of my poetry. I thought of my ambition to write—always to write" (159). D'Angelo will not choose the technical track. He will not be Americanized. And in a sort of twisted, ironic way he becomes alienated from his fellow immigrants precisely so that he can sing their songs, tell their stories of sorrow.

Rosenfeld said that "the outsider often finds himself the perfect insider" (122) and so it was with D'Angelo. Although his desire to write made him a most unusual pick and shovel man, he was the perfect man to show us the Italian immigrant's world. So much of D'Angelo's autobiography tells us just what we might read in a history of Italian immigration, but D'Angelo tells it first hand and with a beautiful, heart-felt grace and courage.

Chapter 3

Immigrant Enigma

In Rome my wife and I visited San Clemente Church. I was especially drawn to an early Christian fresco in the Lower Church excavations depicting the story of Alexius. This son of wealthy parents leaves his family after the marriage ceremony on the day of his wedding. He disappears. Years go by and he returns home, but no one recognizes him and so for some unexplained reason he does not reveal his identity. Instead, he takes a job as a servant, a servant in his own house. He becomes a beloved and trusted servant. Again, years go by and then one day he dies. At his death he holds a sheet of paper so tightly in his hand that only the pope can loosen the fingers and remove the text. They all find out the true identity of this man. But what else has been revealed, I wondered? Why did he do it? And that is precisely what drew me to this story: the unexplainable.

In his chapter on "Narrative in the Poetic Mode" from *Italian Signs, American Streets*, Fred L. Gardaphé titles one section "Pascal D'Angelo's Poesis: Text as Bridge between Cultures." I believe that *Son of Italy* shows a fissure more than it creates a bridge. D'Angelo's narrative does not synthesize the certainties of an ethnic type, the Italian American, but rather it gives us something unknowable, it leaves us with the void that is yesterday. It leaves us wondering why, exactly, did he do it?

Pascal D'Angelo, the Italian immigrant poet "discovered" by Carl Van Doren in the 1920s, worked primarily as a pick-and-shovel man. Yet, despite arriving in America exceedingly poor and unable to speak a word of English, he was determined to become a writer in his adopted land and in his adopted language. He succeeded, though not quite with the Frank-McCourt-farmhouse-in-Connecticut happy ending. D'Angelo published poems in many leading magazines during the early 1920s, and in 1924 Macmillan published his memoir, introduced by Van Doren, *Son of Italy*. This book sold well that year and its author, for a brief moment, became a minor literary celebrity of sorts, but at the same time he remained a pick-and-shovel man. *The Literary Digest* published two portrait essays about D'Angelo: one in 1922 titled "Poet from the Slums" and just three years later, "Triumph of Pascal D'Angelo: Pick and Shovel Poet." *The New York Times* printed a picture of him after his literary success moving a heavy tie on some railroad tracks under construction or repair. He died a few years later—destitute, penniless.

Son of Italy is a remarkable immigrant story. Unlike other such books, D'Angelo's is the story of a writer's struggle to prevail in his chosen art, not to amass riches. It also contradicts the standard notion that Southern Italian immigrants were anti-intellectual, anti-bookish, insular, and provincial.

> Who hears the thuds of the pick and jingling of the shovel? Only the stern-eyed foreman sees me. When night comes and we all quit work the thuds of the pick and the jingling of the shovel are heard no more. All my works are lost, lost forever. But if I write a good line of poetry—then when night comes and I cease writing, my work is not lost. My line is still there. It can be read by you to-day and by another to-morrow. But my pick and shovel works cannot be read either by you to-day or by any one else to-morrow. (74-75)

D'Angelo used poetry and prose to form a non-systematic and ambivalent identity between the old rural folk culture of Southern Italy and the new urban industrial culture of the United States. This conflicted identity remains fluid and unresolved right up to this intriguing and beautiful book's final paragraph.

A brief chronology of D'Angelo's life reads as follows. Born on 20 January 1894 near Introdacqua, a village in the vicinity of the ancient Abruzzi walled city of Sulmona, in 1910 he emigrates with his father to the United States of America, leaving behind in Italy his mother and younger brother. In 1916 his father returns to Italy, young Pascal is now alone. One day in November, 1919 he makes the decision to quit his job with the railroad, move across the river into New York City, and devote himself soley to his literary art. Three years later he has a number of his poems published and two years after that Macmillan publishes his autobiography. Although he did publish other poems in journals such as *The Measure*, the poems listed in the *Readers Guide to Periodical Literature* provide some sense of the sudden and brief trajectory of D'Angelo's career as a poet. In 1922, according to the *Reader's Guide*, he published six poems in five publications; in 1923, two poems in two journals; in 1924, four poems in two places. He published his work in *The Bookman*, *The Century Magazine*, *The Literary Digest*, and *The Nation* among others. On March 17, 1932, he died and a collection had to be initiated by his friends so that he would not be buried in an unmarked grave in a potter's field.

Did the depression throw him out of work in the late 1920s? Even if so, why are there no poems after 1924? In his autobiography D'Angelo says, "I am filled with the urge to cry out, to cry out disconnected words, expressions of pain—anything—to cry out!" (137). Near the climax of his narrative he recalls that "the more things turned against me, the more I stood my ground" (171). William Rose Benet mourned the death of D'Angelo in his *Saturday Review of Literature* column of 26 March 1932 and noted that at his death D'Angelo's final concerns were for his poems, a large sheaf of which had been unpublished. Had he stopped sending them out? He often says in *Son of Italy* that he identified himself as a pick-and-shovel man—and a poet, that he refused to abandon the working-class world after his literary success. He reverses the usual Italian American immigrant characteristics of a distrust of formal education and intense loyalty to one's family, but he does not melt into a stereotypical American in doing so. He also does not return to Italy with his father despite the fact that it is his father's wish that his son accompany him home. *Son of Italy* may be a rather prosaic and uninspiring title in someway, but it is significant for it shows quite clearly that the younger D'Angelo, who stays in America, refused to assimilate.

Some things in this narrative are clear: Pascal D'Angelo, a pick-and-shovel man, has spoken and has been heard. But who is this one who has spoken? It is hard to say exactly because many things are contradictory in *Son of Italy*.

Throughout the book, D'Angelo, in Italian American manner, wages a battle between fate and individual will. At one point of despair, he writes, "I had resigned my-self to my fate. I was a poor laborer—a dago, a wop or some such creature—in the eyes of America. Well, what could I do?" (138). Van Doren, in his autobiography *Three Worlds*, almost takes even this predestined and powerless identity away from D'Angelo. "It has been guessed," he writes, "that he [D'Angelo ...] only ran errands for some knowing writer who used this trick to hoax an editor" (134). Although he says that stories about a D'Angelo hoax are false, he uses a condescending tone and an off-hand style when he speaks of him. In his introduction to *Son of Italy*, he calls the book "delightful" (ix), a seemingly unimaginable, never mind an unsuitable, word to use. In *Three Worlds*, he quickly tosses D'Angelo off: "Pascal D'Angelo taught himself to write and wrote a single book" (134). Gardaphé describes Van Doren pejoratively "as D'Angelo's literary *padrone*" (37). And yet in his three brief writings on D'Angelo—a "Roving Critic" essay, the introduction for *Son of Italy*, and part of one chapter in his autobiography—Van Doren quotes extensively from D'Angelo. In fact, most of the words that Van Doren uses in these writings are D'Angelo's, not his own.

"The literary world began to take me up," D'Angelo says on the last page of his book. "But," he adds,

> more sincere and dearer to my heart were the tributes of my fellow workers who recognized that at last one of them had risen from the ditches and quick-sands of toil to speak his heart to the upper world. (185)

Not everyone was congratulatory, however. *The New York Times* reviewer wondered "what percentage of his subsequent success is due to the mental laziness that makes people judge a work of art by its source rather than on its merits." The reviewer said that *Son of Italy* may be "of sociological interest" and that it is "pleasing rather than profound, interesting rather than significant."

I find it an extraordinary book. It is one-hundred and eighty-five pages long and has fifteen chapters. The pacing and structure of the book propels the reader. It is not haphazard. It begins leisurely with some childhood memories and incidents such as being falsely accused of striking another boy. Then in the second chapter we get the basic facts of date and place of birth. Much of what D'Angelo writes describes well-known facets of Southern Italian and Italian American life, but the way he tells it differs vastly from an immigration historian's way. Consider the poetic prose of the following and specifically D'Angelo's use of alliteration and image:

> The peaks of the azure mountain were barely visible in a mist of heights with their red rifts that seemed to be the unhealed scars left by the storms that rage up there. Only a ruddy cloud was kinging the softened blue above them. (14)

D'Angelo's mountainous rural homeland fosters ancient traditions and in the third chapter he tells the story of the village vampire. It is the longest chapter in the book. It describes young Pascal's several meetings with the vampire and how when a sick village child dies the parents blame her and plot their revenge. This chapter can stand on its own as a fascinating folk narrative.

Chapter four, in contrast, reveals the D'Angelo's family concern with pressing contemporary and immediate matters. It describes their decision to pursue a steady income in America with which to support the family in Italy. Chapter five describes the final days at home, the departure, and the journey of father and eldest son. From agricultural work in a tradition bound village, Pascal and his father travel to Naples via the modern machine, the railroad train. Nothing is simply this or that in *Son of Italy*. Even the ocean voyage D'Angelo describes as "a nightmare, interposed with moments of strange brilliance" (57).

Chapters six through ten describe the various jobs and a few of the adventures that D'Angelo has with his fellow workers, most of whom are also immigrants from the same region in Italy and hence form a sort of family and community for one another in this foreign land. At the end of this section, after the work gang splits and things go from bad to worse, Pascal's father returns to Italy while Pascal begins his long on-again, off-again stretch of working for the railroad and living in a box car. D'Angelo intersperses poems throughout the autobiography, ten in all. Chapter ten, for example, ends with "Accident in the Coal Dump" (inspired by his railroad work) whereas chapter eleven opens with "Omnis Sum" ("I Am All").

Chapter eleven tells how the offer of some road building work in northern New Jersey lured him away from the railroad. Here D'Angelo has a tyrannical foreman:

> The foreman was getting angry that I wiped my face while the others worked bowed with sweat pouring down over them. He snarled that it was just an excuse for raising my bowed body from the continual toil. (121)

In the previous chapter, two members of D'Angelo's gang die when a derrick breaks. This event that reads like a scene from di Donato's *Christ in Concrete* leads to the gang's break up after their four years together. Another di Donato-like scene occurs on the road building job when Pascal must push wheelbarrow after wheelbarrow full of cement up a steep and slippery incline.

> The wheelbarrow dropped down into the foundation. Wildly I threw out my hands and propped myself against the wood-work in order to avoid an inevitable fall. A rusty nail pierced my right hand. And I shrieked. Blood began to come out from both sides of my hand. (124)

After all this, what happens? *La forza del destino*: the contractor had gone bankrupt and everyone on the job goes unpaid.

D'Angelo returns to the railroad yard (chapter twelve) where he resigns himself "to the gradual eking out of my life" (139). Yet, this is also the chapter that he tells of his first writing and his growing interest in literature and language. The following chapter contains a humorous reprieve before the climatic final chapters. The last two chapters describe not only his desire to be a poet and his first submissions of his work to editors, but also the incredible suffering he incurs for his art. These pages move at a very quick pace and are sublimely moving.

Even the lukewarm review in *The New York Times Book Review* recognized one unusual feature of *Son of Italy*. "Pascal D'Angelo," according to the *Times* reviewer, "Is one of that class of men, rare in America, whose success is so spiritual as to be almost entirely devoid of material embellishments." Shortly before the publication of the *Times* evaluation, a reviewer for the *Boston Transcript* also noted this unique feature:

> Among the autobiographies of immigrants which have been fairly frequent of recent years, this of Pascal D'Angelo stands alone because, out of them all, his aim is not to get on and make money and a secure position for himself in this country, but to say something which his very soul felt needed to be said.

More recently William Boelhower finds that "the true meaning of his use of the success-myth convention [...] is to generate a dialogue between the traditional promise of opportunity and the excluded Italian-American type" (128). D'Angelo himself remarks near the riveting conclusion of his book:

> I reflected: what was one little starvation more or less in a man's life, especially in that of a self-anointed poet? Within a few years we would be gone, so why not sing our songs in the meanwhile? (161)

D'Angelo says nothing here of struggle, of deferred gratification leading to fame and fortune and glory. No, he says he'll struggle and starve and then die.

As Robert Orsi has said, some Italian-American immigrants came "to see all accomplishment, worth, and value in terms of making more and more money, a task" to which they applied themselves "with monastic discipline" (*Madonna of 115th Street* 156). But D'Angelo's discipline went to writing, to his art and not to grab at capitalism's gold ring. He criticizes the economics of his homeland once, but he criticizes those of his adopted land several times. "Our people have to emigrate," he writes. "Every bit of cultivable soil is owned by those fortunate few who lord over us" and "land is rented out [...] under usurious conditions [...]" (47). Yet at precisely the same point, D'Angelo recalls that when he first heard of his father's plan to emigrate he thought of America as a "strange place into which people we knew had vanished and never returned" (46). To enter America is to enter the jaws of a monster, the leviathan.

If Italy has its unjust agricultural system, America has an equally unjust industrial system. Specifically, D'Angelo criticizes the high risk and high cost of transportation to a place of employment and the gross ill-practices of the commissary system at a work site. According to D'Angelo:

> High railroad fares are usually what keep laborers near this hell-hole metropolis [New York]. Going to a distant job is a gamble. A man may pay a large part of his scanty savings for fare. And when he gets there he may find living conditions impossible and the foreman too overbearing. (100)

An even greater evil in America for the immigrant than high train ticket prices is the commissary system, the company store that "sold bread, clothes, liquors and other necessities at the most exorbitant prices" (108). "In its most extreme workings," D'Angelo says, the commissary system "results in perpetual peonage of the unlucky laborers" who find at the end of their term of employment "no wages are paid" and that "they themselves are in debt to the company" (111). Nor could one easily fight this system. An employee who tried to save his money instead of spend it in the company store risked losing his job. D'Angelo, who herded sheep as a young boy in Italy, notes that the American industrial system turns men into sheep.

The family for the Italian American immigrant oftentimes acted as antidote to poisonous practices of American business. As Pietro di Donato's protagonist states at the end of *Christ in Concrete*, "Mama. [...] We need each other more than ever—before we die crushed like papa!" (231). The family does not act as buffer in *Son of Italy*. Pascal and his father come to America not for personal gain, but to strengthen their family. This is typical of the Italian American experience. As Orsi writes of immigrants to East Harlem, "The decision to emigrate was a family decision, taken as part of a broader family strategy for survival" and the goal of this strategy was "to strengthen and preserve the family" (*Madonna of 115th Street* 18). The D'Angelo family experience partially corresponds to this pattern. At first, just the father plans to seek a better income in America *for his family in Italy*. Then, as a family, they decide that sixteen-year-old Pascal should also go: "our blessing would be double if I went, or else we would return in half the time and all be together again" (50).

Pascal D'Angelo's narrative, his experience, does not fit the Italian American pattern after this point. Orsi claims that "as long as important segments of an immigrant's family remained in the mezzogiorno, Italy absorbed that immigrant's attention [...]" (*Madonna of 115th Street* 19). Pascal's younger brother and mother remained in Italy, yet he never mentions his brother after arriving in America and he says very little of his mother. In fact, he almost never mentions his father either who is the one immediate family member with him. Whereas Pascal was distraught when first told his father would soon leave for America, he says very little about his father's departure from America back to Italy. Instead of weeping he recalls that "there was a lingering suspicion that somewhere in this vast country an opening existed, that somewhere I would strike the light" (115).

Pascal D'Angelo's story does not exactly typify the conflict between American individualism and Italian family loyalty. *Son of Italy* explores rather than resolves this aspect of the Italian American experience. In someway the work gang becomes Pascal's new family, but the vicissitudes of the American system tear apart the gang comprised of other men from Abruzzi. D'Angelo, who only once mentions homesickness for Italy (132), seems to forget his family in Introdacqua, loses his family of fellow workers from the same region in Italy, but remains loyal to the larger family of the immigrant laborer. He does not pursue material wealth for darling narcissistic self, but yearns "to express all the sorrows of those who cower under the crushing yoke of an unjust doom" (181).

The story of D'Angelo's self-education and his love for learning and language reveals another aspect of *Son of Italy* that renders it profound, significant, and unusual among immigrant autobiographies. The Italian immigrant, we are often told, had a high illiteracy rate and expressed a fear that too much education would lead to desires impossible to fulfill. Even as recently as the 1970s Richard Gambino could truthfully write that "Italian-Americans up to now have been a group that did not read" (*Blood of My Blood* 270). Lucia Santa in Mario Puzo's *The Fortunate Pilgrim* worries about her daughter Octavia because she loves to go to school and read books that import to Octavia "American airs." Lucia "distrusted high ambition, high aims. For, the greater the reward, it followed, the greater the risks. [...] Better a modest safety" (139). In contrast to this hesitancy was the feeling that "America was not Italy." "In America," Puzo says, "you could escape your destiny" (267). D'Angelo, who sought artistic success and remained loyal to the brotherhood of laborers, uniquely describes his experience in the borderland between a reverence for traditions and an attempt through education to escape the bounds of fate.

Gardaphé argues that for the early Italian immigrant authors, including D'Angelo, "control of language [...] means greater control of the self as American" (*Italian Signs, American Streets* 36). Furthermore, he says that, "acquiring the ability to signify the immigrant experience would become the key to shifting from the powerlessness of an oral culture ruled by destiny to a written culture in which one could exercise greater control over one's life" (27). I don't believe these are either / or matters for D'Angelo. For example, even as he gains literacy in English and some control over his life, he still retains a belief in the power of fate and an appreciation for oral culture. He does not exactly reject the country side (oral culture) for the urban (print culture), either. At one point he says of New York, "how lovely and yet repulsive this enchanted city was" (84). Clearly, this shows the ambivalence that he felt.

Early in his book he tells us that his parents, unlike some others in the area, could not read or write and that he learned more from listening to his elders (oral culture) than from school (print culture) (19). "By the time I was twelve," he recalls, "I stopped going to school entirely and began my life of continuous toil" (21). While working with fellow townsmen upon arrival in America offered a certain comfort and familiarity to life in a new and strange land, it also hindered any desire for advancement through education. "None of us, including myself, ever thought of a movement to broaden our knowledge of the English language. [...] We formed our own little world [...]" (70).

D'Angelo, of course, eventually does learn English, but rather than provide a systematic treatise on the benefits of language acquisition he explores the unsettled and contradictory nature of the relationship between power and language. Nor can it be stated simply that acquisition of English corresponds to assimilation to American individualism and urban industrial life whereas retention of one's native language corresponds to insular group solidarity and a connectedness to a rural existence ruled by a belief in inescapable fate.

In one of the most memorable passages regarding language acquisition D'Angelo describes how he triumphed over a group of "Americans" in a word contest (146-147).[1] Yet, soon after this memory of pride and power through language he records a dialogue regarding the efficacy of

---

[1] At the end of the century Louise DeSalvo recalls in her memoir *Vertigo* a similar contest. "I was a girl, too young for school, very small for my age, and working-class and Italian. In the eyes of the world, I wasn't worth much, and wouldn't amount to anything." Against a "dirty little boy" who makes fun of her last name and torments her, she "used the weapon of words, the only ones in my arsenal, but they were already considerable" (77).

his newly formed skills. "I became the cause of considerable argument among my fellow-workers. Some maintained that my knowledge of English would help me to advance in this world and others insisted that a man who was born a laborer could never rise" (158). An elderly worker, Felice, says, "'And you, who they say can write English—what good does it do you [...]'" (159). He advises Pascal to abandon manual labor and seek an office job. D'Angelo, who when he first begins to write seems to fish about for a language in which to write and starts his first composition in Italian "but unable to manage the language" decides "to attempt it in English" (141), will not abandon pick and shovel culture nor will he seek special favor from his elite literary acquaintances. He is adamant about this in his correspondence to Van Doren, and William Rose Benet in his review of *Son of Italy* says that much of the book surprised him for he knew D'Angelo for several years before its publication and although he was aware that D'Angelo did not have an easy life, he did not know how tough the circumstances of his friend's life were for D'Angelo never asked for so much as a slice of bread.

Another way that D'Angelo expresses ambivalence about the power over destiny provided by literacy can be seen in his comments regarding city versus country life. If American language proficiency acts as a key to the city, to modern American urban life, then once one enters that door the old ways of rural life should be left behind. Again, this rigid pattern does not precisely fit D'Angelo's narrative. While at the beginning of chapter twelve he says, "I felt a kinship with the beautiful earth" (137), near the start of chapter fourteen he says, "as I walked through its [New York's] crowded streets, I felt a sort of kinship with it" (161). And yet in a poem inserted in this latter place in his narrative he says that "the souls of many who speed [...] / are dim with storms," but "the soul of a farm lad who plods [...] / Is a bright blue sky" (160). In his poem "The City" that New York inspired he writes:

> The factory smoke is unfolding in protesting curves
> Like phantoms of black unappeased desires, yearning and
>   struggling and pointing upward;

> While through its dark streets pass people, tired, useless,
> Trampling the vague black illusions
> That pave their paths [...] (163)

Perhaps, the belief that control of language means control of fate is one of those "vague black illusions" for in the American system as in the Italian (literate or illiterate) escaping one's destiny will be difficult if not impossible. Consider D'Angelo's description of a factory town just outside New York City.

> It has nothing but factories and workingmen's shacks. How many of them are to be found all over the country! Towns of filthy hovels, towns of congested quarters and unhealthy conditions, all of them, little miniature East Sides and Mulberry Bends, scattered among the green stretches and broad open spaces of America. And over each of them, feeding upon them, looms the ever-present factory or mill. (79)

When D'Angelo first arrived in America he misread street signs. In a humorous passage he notes, "'Ave.! Ave.! Ave.!' How religious a place this must be that expresses its devotion at every crossing, I mused" (61). He does learn how to read and write "American" English, but learning how to read a culture does not necessarily equate with gaining full entrance to it.

Language does not provide entry to the urban industrial citadel of power for Pascal D'Angelo. Either by choice or fate, he stays forever a pick-and-shovel man. He does not escape destiny. Louis Podesta, the character in Louis Forgione's autobiographical novel *Reamer Lou*, says,

> I have always lived on the threshold. I have never known the real America, the America of those who rise, of those whose minds and souls are uplifted from the darkness of ignorance and superstition. I've always lived among these immigrants who fell or, at the best, made no progress. (258)

To some extent, so it was for Forgione's friend Pascal D'Angelo. (The factory town that D'Angelo describes on page seventy-nine is the same one that serves as the setting for Forgione's novel *The River Between*.)

Although at one point he can say that "without realizing it, I had learned the great lesson of America: I had learned to have faith in the future" (171), shortly afterwards he states very bleakly at the end of a poem titled "Light" that suffering "is the price of a forbidden dream sunken in the / purple sea of an obscure future" (179). The one thing he knew for certain about his "obscure future" was that he would always be a pick-and-shovel man. "I was and am a pick and shovel man. That's all I am able to do, and that is what I am forced to do, even now," i.e., after the years 1922-1924 and his limited but significant literary success (145). At the end of his narrative he declares that he is "not deserting the legions of toil to refuge myself in the literary world." Rather, he sought a means "to express all the sorrows of those who cower under the crushing yoke of an unjust doom" (181) and that would include the author himself, a pick-and-shovel man.

Pascal D'Angelo did not write to melt into an Anglo world. His story is not John Fante's *The Road to Los Angeles*, a story of an Italian American boy, Arturo Gabriel Bandini, who wants to be a writer, and when this boy first writes something he composes a fantasy about himself as a wealthy WASP named, "Arthur Banning, the multi-millionaire oil-dealer, tour de force, prima facies, petit maitre, table d'hote, and great lover of ravishing, beautiful, exotic, saccharine, and constellation-like women in all parts of the world, in every corner of the globe" (130) and so on. Those were not the dreams of Pascal D'Angelo. Nor did he take care of practical business in the manner Anthony Julian Tamburri suggests for the Italian American writer: "First, there was the need to establish economic security in order to enable the development of a writing discipline" (24). Instead, D'Angelo quits his job and becomes what contemporary American novelist Paul Auster has called a "hunger artist."

In his essay "The Art of Hunger," Auster explains the self-imposed regimen of Norwegian novelist Knut Hamsun's protagonist in *Hunger* (1890) as follows: "His fast [...] is a contradiction. To persist in it would mean death, and with death the fast would end" (13). In the course of his fast Hamsun's protagonist, according to Auster, will "systematically unburden himself of every belief in every system, and in the end by means of the hunger he has inflicted upon himself, he arrives at nothing. There is nothing to keep him going—and yet he keeps going" (20).[2] So it is in the final pages of Pascal D'Angelo's *Son of Italy*.

As noted earlier, in November, 1919 D'Angelo makes the "hasty" but momentous decision to quit his job, move across the river, and devote himself fully to his art. He announces his decision to a fellow worker who tells him, "'you will starve'." And D'Angelo replies, "'I shall'" (160-161). He does not deny it, he embraces it: "what was one little starvation more or less in a man's life, especially in that of a self-anointed poet? Within a few years we would be gone, so why not sing our songs in the meanwhile?" (161). This quotation shows that although D'Angelo takes an individual action for the sake of his art, he still associates himself with the larger group in which he maintains a sort of membership in absentia. Although he will write his poems, he writes here of "our songs," showing a continued affinity for oral culture even as he seeks to enter print. He takes charge of his own destiny when he quits the railroad yard, but he realizes ultimate things remain out of his or anyone else's control: "within a few years we would be gone." Lastly, he does not say that he will struggle and through hard work and deferred gratification he will attain fame and fortune. No, he will simply struggle and starve.

And things do move in a downward spiral to a near death zero point. "I went to live in the cheapest hole that I could find. [...] Having little money left I set out to master the situation. The easiest thing to cut was food" (168-169). His final privation comes when a thief steals his last few pennies from his ragged coat pockets while he is at the New York Public Library. When he leaves the library for home and reaches for subway fare he realizes what has happened. He decides to walk home to Brooklyn from Fifth Avenue and Forty-Second Street. He figures the

---

[2] Auster recalls his own experiences of "hunger" in his memoir *Hand to Mouth*.

hike will take him no more that three and one-half hours. As he approaches Canal Street in lower Manhattan, it begins to rain. Then the rain turns to sleet. He is soaked. When he reaches his hovel he sees that snow and rain have poured into his unheated room through a window that some neighborhood children had pried open. But it gets worse. The pipes in the communal bathroom adjacent to his room had burst, spewing forth filth all over the floor of his meager habitation. He awakes the next morning "aching and coughing, with fits of fever" (176). Yet, he continues.

Curiously, the book ends with mention of his parents. He hardly ever mentions them at all after his arrival in America, and yet in the very last paragraph he writes of "the happiness of my parents who realized that after all I had not really gone astray" (185).[3] Although in the penultimate paragraph he says that despite his recent literary successes his fellow workers are still dear to him, in the last paragraph he says he "sought and attained a goal far from the deep-worn groove of peasant drudgery" (185). These words do not resolve any issues of the Italian American immigrant experience, but rather explore the ambivalent and contradictory nature of that experience.

D'Angelo's autobiography is not simple in its trajectory. Life seldom goes in the straightforward manner imagined by ghost-writers; at least, not while it is being lived. No, life is perhaps like a web in which we are caught, a web lacking a center. We step forward and backward. Everything blends into everything and nothing can ever with certainty be defined. D'Angelo's autobiography is a non-systematic, unsettled, and contradictory text.[4] It is the story of an artist, not a capitalist. I do not see how it could not fascinate anyone who is or who has ever wished to be a

---

[3] Albanese writing of her grandfather Frank Spiziri says that "to be a poet and artist would be to neglect his family duty. Yet, paradoxically, performing himself a poet would catapult Spiziri into the ranks of the *galantuomini* [gentlemen] where his father and elder brother, Daniel, had already found a place. And the rank he secured would surely reflect on family honor" (42).

[4] Even D'Angelo's place of origin exists in a sort of borderland. It lies just north of the Mezzogiorno's boundary, but certainly has never shared in the North's wealth.

writer. At one point late in his struggle for publication, D'Angelo humorously rationalizes that if George Washington was such an able general, then two George Washington stamps on a submission envelope should be able to storm the gate of any editor's fortress (163).

Chapter 4

ANGER AND ASSIMILATION IN NEW YORK

Louis Forgione attended New York City public schools and then spent three years at the College of the City of New York. He withdrew from his studies after his father's failed health made it necessary for him to undertake full time employment (Peragallo 105). Despite this change of fortune, Louis Forgione wrote three noteworthy novels published by E. P. Dutton in the 1920s: *Reamer Lou* (1924), *The Men of Silence* (1928), and *The River Between* (1928). Two of these long out-of-print novels are stories of urban Italian American immigrant life and the limits of assimilation. *Reamer Lou*, for example, begins: "I have always considered myself a sort of half-and-half foreigner, though I was born and brought up in America" (1). Indeed, Constantine Panunzio, author of the well-known immigrant autobiography *Soul of an Immigrant* published by Macmillan in 1921, said in the review essay of this novel: "Whether with conscious purpose or by divine accident the author has presented the first authentic picture, in fiction form, of the American-born child of immigrants and herein lies the social significance of this volume." In *The River Between*, Forgione charts some economic progress for his characters, but this progress does not come easily and it takes place beyond the bounds of the city, across the river on the New Jersey side. The social rise in this novel results in the near disintegration of the family: a bitter father, a son whose wife leaves him. *The River Between* is a near-prophetic novel in that it anticipates much that will be developed in more current Italian American literature. The character of an enraged father who cannot speak to his children as seen in urban Italian American novels such as Dorothy Calvetti Bryant's *Miss Giardino* and Josephine Gattuso Hendin's *The Right Thing to Do* has its antecedent in Forgione's character Demetrio, an immigrant worker who succeeds in establishing his own construction firm but nonetheless feels betrayed by the dream of success and uses his anger to beat down his son and daughter-in-law.

It is my contention that throughout the history of Italian American writing from D'Angelo and Forgione through di Donato and Fante to Bryant and Hendin or even to a young contemporary writer like Nicholas Montemarano anger is not repressed but oftentimes quite explicitly and sometimes quite loudly expressed. Andrew Rolle asserts, "It is my belief that immigrants concealed their resentments through a form of self-burial, but that anger had to be defended against by passivity and conformity" (38). It is my belief that characters such as Louis Podesta in Forgione's *Reamer Lou* or Rose Lyba in his *The River Between* or Anna Giardino in Bryant's novel or Gina Giardello in Hendin's *The Right Thing to Do* express their anger and through their very assertive actions reject conformity. Whereas Fred L. Gardaphé has said that "the children of Italian immigrants used their writing both to document and to escape the conditions under with they were born and raised" (*Italian Signs, American Streets* 57), I emphasize that they used it to protest those conditions.

Whereas Helen Barolini in her "Introduction" to *The Dream Book* says that "More than men, the displacement from one culture to another has represented a real crisis of identity for the woman of the Italian family [...]" (19), Mario Puzo tells us in *The Fortunate Pilgrim* that "It was always the men who crumbled under the glories of the new land, never the women" (107). Despair: it's a not a contest. Edward Corsi, who for a number of years served as United State Commissioner, Immigration and Naturalization, New York District, describes the difficulties that both his mother and his stepfather faced in America. His mother, he says, "loved quiet, and hated noise and confusion." In New York City, he continues, "she spent her days, and the waking hours of the nights sitting at that one outside window staring up at the little patch of sky above the tenements" (23). After three years in New York, she returned to Italy where she died the following year. "America," Corsi states, "had failed to offer its pot of gold. It had offered instead suffering, privations, and defeat" (27). Though his stepfather remained in America, his "bondage in the piano factory literally crushed him for the rest of his life [...]" (27).

My point here is that the privations experienced by immigrants and immigrants' reactions to those privations can be divided along gender lines only with a reductionism of the true experience, only by rendering a complex experience simple. Robert Orsi describes much of this complexity in *The Madonna of 115th Street*. He observes, for example, that while the mother in the family provided the center, these "powerful women of the community were expected to show an absolute respect for their husbands and sons in public, even though everyone in the community knew that such subservience was theater" (133).

In *The River Between* Demetrio, his son Orestes, and his daughter-in-law Rose, are all, at times, very angry at their situation in America, in New York City and directly across the river in Shady Side, New Jersey. This anger and the complexities of immigration and assimilation from which it emerges are not just the stuff of fiction or of only the early twentieth-century. Anna Giardino in Dorothy Bryant's 1978 novel *Miss Giardino* realizes at the story's end that one thing she shares with her angry immigrant father is, quite simply, anger. A recent immigrant to the United States, R. Radhakrishnan, asks in an essay titled "Is the Ethnic 'Authentic' in the Diaspora?"

> How could some*one* be both *one* and something *other*? How could the unity of identity have more than one face or name? If my son is both Indian and American, which *one* is he *really*? Which is the real self and which the other? How do these two selves coexist and how do they weld into one identity? How is ethnic identity related to national identity? Is this relationship hierarchically structured, such that the "national" is supposed to subsume and transcend ethnic identity, or does this identity produce a hyphenated identity [...]? (204)

Whereas Gino Speranza, the son of immigrants from Verona, Italy, published his treatise on these questions, *Race or Nation*, in 1923, Radhakrishnan's essay appears in a book published in 1996.

In both fiction and more recently in scholarship it has been noted that this *one* that after immigration becomes *two*, itself and another, oftentimes emerges as a very conflicted and insecure individual. Some years ago Jerre Mangione noted: "works of literature, usually written by the offspring of the immigrants, often reveal that fundamental aspect of ethnic life which is either glossed over or ignored by scholars—that is, the psychological dilemma of the ethnic as he or she tries to cope with the conflicts of a dualistic existence" ("A Double Life" 171). Mangione claimed that "growing up in a bi-cultural situation [...] inevitably created feelings of conflict and guilt" and led to "psychic distress" ("A Double Life" 174).

A brief example from fiction that illustrates this "psychic distress" can be found at the start of Barolini's 1979 novel *Umbertina* when Marguerite tells her psychoanalyst that her father tried to make himself "into a real American." She says that "he was caught in a terrible trap; he couldn't be either Italian like his father and mother or American like his models without feeling guilty toward one or the other side" (19). This guilt, Marguerite observes, leads to shame, "conflict and bitterness" (19).

Rolle's 1980 study *The Italian Americans: Troubled Roots* promises in its introduction to examine this psychic trap, but the promise goes largely unfulfilled as he turns in later chapters to a sort of ethnic pride boosterism. In his introduction he claims that "historians have troweled over emotional disabilities" of the immigrants (xiii). The immigrants, Rolle says, repressed their emotional difficulties so that they could better adapt to American life. But, he adds, "their repressions proved damaging for some of them" (xv). Unfortunately, Rolle's confused book abandons its thesis and its support and rambles into and on such Italian American commonplaces as "A Touch of the Gutter: La Mafia and

Crime," as he titles one chapter, or as another is titled, perhaps the formers' opposite, "Making It Big and Small."[1]

A far better foray into this psychological distress of immigrants and their offspring is an essay by Mary Ann Mannino. Mannino examines the trauma of immigration and the generational transfer of this trauma. She convincingly reads Rita Ciresi's *Blue Italian* and Barolini's *Umbertina* to show how "the progeny of immigrants often manifest symptoms of depression and anxiety [...]" (6). Mannino's analysis, however, looks only at mothers and daughters and does not consider that in addition to anxiety anger might also be expressed (not repressed).

In addition to the trauma of immigration and the transference of this trauma to the children of immigrants, another reason for this expressed anger, especially in the 1920s, was the virulent attack on immigrants by many people in America. These attacks came not only from the pens of Puritans or Yankees. Constantine Panunzio, for example, observed that in the late 1920s, "Immigrants or the children of immigrants turned against their own people, as is the case of the vituperative attack made by Gino Speranza [...]" (114). In his 1927 plea for moderation, *Immigration Crossroads*, Panunzio bemoaned that in this decade "Immigrants were categorically and continuously assailed, and life became difficult and heartrending even to the best of them" (115).

Whereas Panunzio objected to unfairness in American immigration policy of the 1920s, Speranza quite bluntly advocated a complete end to all immigration. As he put it in *Race or Nation*, "We must abolish 'the immigrant' from our minds and from our lives; from our polity and from our policies" (254).[2] Even if all immigration were to cease, America

---

[1] "What do the 'famous' Italian Americans stand for?" Barolini asks in her essay "Buried Alive by Language": "Money and celebrity status. Not much uplift there, not much for the soul of alienated and ambivalent people to feed on. No gut nourishment" (*Chiaroscuro* 66).

[2] During World War I, Speranza, an American-born lawyer specializing in international and immigration law, worked as a war correspondent in Italy for the *New York Evening Post*. After the war he stayed in Italy, assisting the American embassy. His negative experience of anti-Americanism in post war Italy caused him to reconsider his previous

would still confront an almost insurmountable dilemma according to Speranza, "the problem of the millions who are not, in fact and in cultural and spiritual essentials, 'American,' though in law they are declared so to be" (256-257). Foreign born naturalized citizens could be citizens in law but not in fact because America is "first and above all [...] the development, essentially, of Anglo-Saxon ways of thinking and doing, and, more specifically, of New England ideas and ideals" ("Does Americanization Americanize?" 267).[3] To those who argued that immigrants and naturalized citizens have enriched the American experience, Speranza replied,

> There has been a great deal of finely-phrased nonsense and spurious scholarship as to the 'contribution' of our immigrant masses to American culture and American civilization. [...] As a matter of fact and of history, culture is not 'carried' from one civilized country into another 'by way of Ellis Island.' Indeed the inflow into any civilization of large masses of alien peoples, especially of the peasant class as most of our best immigrants have been, never did, and never can contribute to the culture of the nation that receives them. (152)

Recently, Matthew Frye Jacobson has described how in the late nineteenth and early twentieth-century Americans "recognized biologically based 'races' rather than culturally based 'ethnicities'" and so "one might be both white *and* racially distinct from other whites" (6). These various "races" that today we call "ethnicities" had to learn, he says, how to become white: "the civic assimilation (the process by which the Irish, Russian Jews, Poles, and Greeks became Americans) is inseparable from the cultural story or racial alchemy (the process by which

---

pluralistic views of immigration and assimilation when he returned to New York in 1919.

[3] Because the United States is primarily Anglo-Saxon in origin and is the fruit of Anglo-Saxon democratic traditions, Speranza argues, Italians, who only recently formed a democratic nation, are unfit for participatory democracy. In her essay "Tainted Soil" Maria Laurino provides a contemporary look at this decades old anti-Italian American argument.

Celts, Hebrews, Slavs, and Mediterraneans became Caucasians)" (8). The 1920s, according to Frye, was the watershed decade when "the late nineteenth century's probationary white groups were now remade and granted the scientific stamp of authenticity as the unitary Caucasian race [...]" (8). However, the many different views expressed on "race" and "nation" in the 1920s show that this remaking and granting was neither a smooth nor a unitary process.

Pascal D'Angelo dedicated *Son of Italy* to "Luigi Forgione." Louis Forgione, on the other hand, dedicated his 1924 book, *Reamer Lou*, to Walter Littlefield.[4] D'Angelo, whose autobiography does not move much beyond the Italian community in America, Italianizes Forgione's first name. Yet, in a brief profile published in *The Bookman* the following year, Forgione is described as having "light complexion, with dark hair and brown eyes. He looks as though he might be part French" (126). The English journal, *The Bookman*, seems to want to anglicize the author, to push his Southern European ancestry farther north.

One might recall that in Fante's famous story "The Odyssey of a Wop" (1933) the autobiographically based narrator tries to pass as French so that he might be more readily accepted at the school he attends. He says, "[...] when people ask me my nationality, I tell them I am French" (136). He adds, "I thank God for my light skin and hair, and I choose my friends by the Anglo-Saxon ring of their names" (137).

---

[4] D'Angelo's dedication reads: "This book is dedicated to Mr. Luigi Forgione whose aid and encouragement have made its appearance possible." And Forgione's dedication reads: "Dedicated by the author with the greatest respect and esteem to his friend Walter Littlefield." It was Littlefield who provided Forgione with the necessary papers to write *The Men of Silence*. In his foreword to the book Littlefield compliments Forgione's narrative skills. He adds, "Aside from his grasp of the essentials of constructive narrative and his poetic gift of assimilation and delineation, Mr. Forgione possessed an intimate knowledge of Naples and an acquaintance with persons who could check up the police and judicial reports in the light of actual experience [...]" (xxiv), and so Littlefield gave his cache of documents relating to the Neapolitan Camorra and the Cuocolo murders to Forgione. I do not comment in this chapter on Forgione's crime novel. I believe it is his weakest work and would be of interest only to contemporary readers who have an overly enthusiastic appreciation for Italian American crime fiction.

Forgione's first novel seems an exemplar of multi-cultural understanding. The main character, Louis Podesta, has two best friends: one is French Canadian: the other, Lithuanian. The docks and shipyards where Louis works are populated by individuals of all the many immigrant groups that came through Ellis Island and Louis gets along with all of them, for the most part, except for Poles whom he always refers to as "dirty Polacks" (32). Similarly, Edward Corsi had very clear limits to his New Deal liberalism. For Corsi, "John Chinaman" represented the inscrutable other. "John Chinaman," he says, "will always remain for me anthropology's greatest enigma" (176). Immigration inspectors, however, he tells us, had developed a test on which "hinged the Oriental's fate": "the walking test" [...]

> If he is a native Chinaman, he usually lifts his feet in perpendicular fashion. If American born, he kicks his feet forward in the genuine Yankee manner. This interesting test is predicated on the theory that the Chinese who have worked in their native rice fields, have worn sandals all their lives and have formed the habit of lifting their feet in perpendicular fashion. (164)

But no test, Corsi says, can be perfect due to "the weird, innate cleverness of the Chinaman [...]" (163).

Louis Podesta rejects the attentions of the Italian woman, Annie, who pursues him and, in turn, he pursues Mary Andersen, the foreman's daughter. Rose Lyba abandons her Italian husband in order to have an affair with Arthur Halstead, a tin-pan alley composer. Mary rejects Louis precisely because he is the son of southern European immigrants. Mary tells Louis near the end of their relationship: "'You know it is almost a sacrifice for me to go out with you—a favor I am doing you. [...] You know what people think about your race of whom you represent the very lowest and vulgar class'" (131). At the end of *The River Between* Rose decides to leave Manhattan and return to the Italian community on the New Jersey side of the river, not so much to rejoin her husband as to take care of her father-in-law. Yet, her last words, the last words of the novel, she speaks in her contemporary Americanized jazzy diction.

"'Like fun!'" she exclaims (254). She means by this that she won't be returning to Manhattan anytime soon. But can we believe her, this "'noisy, Americanized'" brat of a plodding "'Wop',," (39) as she describes herself near the start of the novel? Do her final words betray or intimate a betrayal of her final action?

If ethnicity is mutable, if the attractions of Americanization are also repulsive and offensive, then so too is the space of ethnicity and the space of Americanization. It is mutable and it is both attractive and repulsive. New York City has been praised with endless city pride, but also condemned in sharp critique. From seventeenth century Dutch burghers to present day mayors Giuliani and Bloomberg the message presented to the world is that New York City is a place of compassion and tolerance and its people, a people of unique and exceptional ability. As the song says, "If I can make it here, I can make it anywhere."[5]

Italian American authors, contrarily, offer a very harsh critique of this metropolis. D'Angelo calls it a "hell-hole" (100) and in his poem entitled "The Toilers" he describes a laborer's torment:

> Throughout the night you are hurled
> In a confused heave of struggling illusions,
> Under the machinal flights of those moistened
>   walls,
> Under those black, moistened walls of disregarded
>   futility.
> Facing this Giant monument of bitterness –
> Your thoughts!
> Amid the incessant whirrs of the maniac motors,
> Are smashed into fragments of an irresolved
>   dream,
> And you are swept on! On!

---

[5] For a recent view that differs from the pro-New York marketing campaigns see Montemarano's *A Fine Place*. This is a novel about a family that has not made it in America. Read page 106 and keep in mind those television slogans about history and diversity. As it says on page 155, "There was [is?] no such thing as a fine place."

This is not the Jazz Age. This is not F. Scott and Zelda in a fountain at the Plaza Hotel. At Ellis Island, Corsi explains near the end of his memoir, "The incoming were often buoyed as much by false promises as by high hopes; the outgoing frequently bore the earmarks of human treachery as well as the shadow of shattered illusions" (281).

Shortly before his death, Nazone, Paul's godfather in di Donato's *Christ in Concrete*, yearns, as he hugs his godson, "'But oh, that I may leave this land of disillusion!'" (212).[6] After Nazone's death, after his uncle's crushed legs, after his father's death and his own exhausting child labor at age twelve, Paul concludes, "'I only know that I am cheated'" (230). As one character puts it earlier in the novel, "'Vomit your poison, you miserable bastards, for when you go to scratch the louse from your hungry faces you will not even possess the luxury of fingernails'" (77).

But the bright lights of New York do hold out the promise of luxury to all who look in the glare. As Josephine Gattuso Hendin says in her 1980s story *The Right Thing to Do*, "Were you thirsty? The city was water. Were you low? It was all height and promise" (75). But it is also "a mirage" (75). For "at work, every day, in the city, typing past-due bills, or letters politely requesting payment, the beauty of it receded before the familiar routine of drudge-work" (76).

One way to escape drudgery is to associate with anything Anglo and that association usually means a rejection of the self. If this is what Jacobson means by learning how to become white or Speranza by Americanization, then it is not a joyful process. Gina's father, Nino, says at the start of Hendin's novel that his daughter "'wants to be one of them'" (an Anglo) (24). Gina's boyfriend is a fair-skinned, light haired college dropout named Alex whose father is an American historian with a specialty in

---

[6] Pietro di Donato never mentions the words New York City in his novel. His hybrid metropolis is mostly Manhattan but partly Union City, New Jersey. The Molov's (Ducoff's) stationary store, for example, in actuality was in Union City while the building site where Nazone dies is in Manhattan, the West Side Mercedes Benz building—and in the real world this building is only four or five stories high not twenty-five as in the novel.

the Puritans. Gina learns how to negotiate Italian ways and "American" ways, but her education does not come free of brutality and nightmare.

"The myth that told us we could and should be equally American in the Anglo mold," Barolini has noted, "but forgot to mention that to force people to become what they are not produces not equality but enmity—enmity with one's self" ("Introduction" 21). Gina must wrestle with self-rancor, as must Anna Giardino, Louis Podesta, and the members of the Lyba family. During her conversation with Victor, Alex's American historian father, she says, "'To defeat the enemy you have to see through his eyes, become him, think like him. The more you do, the more you lose yourself, your moral bearings'" (142). Gina realizes that what she has said may apply more to her self than to any one else. In this novel situated and written in the 1980s, not in the early twentieth century as *The River Between*, its author explores Italian American identity, its intersection with a perceived dominant American culture, the despair that results from the failure of this connection, and the anger that results from despair.[7]

Anna Giardino realizes at the end of her story that she had intended to burn down the high school where she had taught for many years. She planned to burn down the school because she believed that the promise of America had failed her and her students. This made her angry, and she realizes how very similar her life had been to her immigrant father's. She tells her friend David, "'I felt defeated, when I retired. And angry. Mad. I think of all those years when I used to correct papers, marking "wrong word" in the margin when my students used "mad" to mean "angry." But they were right. Anger is a kind of madness. My father was mad with anger. So was I'" (155).

---

[7] Maria Mazziotti Gillan's poem of the 1980s, "Public School No. 18: Paterson, New Jersey," attacks the injustices of a forced and prejudicial Americanization and it ends: My anger spits / venomous from my mouth. // I am proud of my mother, / dressed all in black, / proud of my father / with his broken tongue, / proud of the laughter / and the noise of my house. // Remember me, ladies, / the silent one? / I have found my voice / and my rage will blow / your house down.

Louis Podesta is quick to use his fists. An aunt in Scranton, Pennsylvania raises Louis after his immigrant father dies in a mining accident and as a young man Louis decides to seek his fortunes in New York City. *Reamer Lou* recounts his two and one-half years of "trouble around New York" and ends with his return to Scranton, "disillusioned, disgusted, wounded" (2). At one shipyard on Staten Island where he works as a reamer (reaming "is the art of making a round hole in a few layers of steel" [6]) and two in Brooklyn where he works as a longshoreman and then as a pipe fitter, he fights. He fights because he doesn't like what the city-as-leviathan does to him or his friends. By the end of the novel he wants to strike out against the entire city, "a fierce blaze burst out in me," he says, "against the whole damned city [...]" (273). He rages against the entire metropolis, "If you were a man I would choke your thick neck and throw you down and spit in your eye" (274). The people who live in New York City, he says, are worse than the city itself. "They're timid," he says, "and always scared of not doing what is commanded of them whether it be right or wrong. [...] Their god is profit. [...] Rotten they are, brokers and speculators and cheaters [...]" (274).

The immigrants, however, are good people turned bad by what happens to them here. "I know what I'm talking about," he says when describing what he calls the tragedy of immigration. "I've seen too many fine young men go bad and decay after a few years in this country. They lose their health, they lose their self-respect, their morality, their restraining Old World customs—those valuable growths of centuries" (97). Three chapters later he echoes these words, these beliefs, these facts as his friend Charlie rots in a hospital: "and that's just it," he says, "—how fine young fellows from the other side are thrown into this country with the bad roads open wide and the good roads shut tight. Few are the ones lucky enough to escape. The rest are slaughtered body and soul. And they rot—and they rot!" (118).

Reamer Lou is a novel about friendship as well as the urban adventures and defeats of one man, a child of immigrants. Charlie had twice told Louis to leave the city, to seek a kinder life in far distant forests. But

Louis doesn't follow Charlie's wishes even after he had promised to do so. For a moment near the end of the story things start looking up for Louis in New York. He has been invited to enter into partnership with a cousin who has prospered in the trucking business and planned to enlarge his successful enterprise into excavation work. Louis says: "My view of America was broadened when I met my cousin Vito" (259). But this broadened view dies quickly, this promise too goes unfulfilled for just as Louis feels "a new hope opening up before" him (261), his other friend, Frank, dies when a poorly constructed platform breaks and sends Frank six feet down onto a live electrical power grid.

Frank's death is, perhaps, slightly more complex than a similar fatal construction accident in *Christ in Concrete*. Louis and Frank had been arguing on this flimsy platform about the formers' attraction to and flirtation with the latter's girl, Helene. But like the accident in *Christ in Concrete* that horribly ends the life of Paul's father, corporate corruption causes the work site death and the rotten corruption continues afterwards, too. In *Christ in Concrete* Fred Murdin, for whom Paul's father, Geremio, worked as a master bricklayer and work gang foreman, criticizes Italian workers at a death claim hearing (132) and yet it was Geremio who warned Murdin "that the underpinning should be doubled and the old material removed from the floors" (5). But Murdin didn't listen to him and kept "the inspector drunk [...]" (5) and drank "from a large bottle of whiskey and cursed in American words [...]" (11). In *Reamer Lou* the assistant superintendent, who "was known to be a rat," asks to have a private conversation with Louis after Frank's death. He says:

> "You see—that man—what's his name—Frank Le Rallec, was electrocuted. And we expect his folks to put up a big howl and sue for a large sum of money. Now you were the only one near him at the time. If you can testify that he fell through some kind of neglect on his part—say that he stepped out too far, or tried some stunt, we'll be saved a lot of money and, of course, we will—" (271)

Before management can offer its bribe, Louis answers with his fists and sends the man, severely beaten, to the hospital. The police issue a warrant for Louis's arrest, and since, as Louis says, "the law was swift-acting against an insignificant person" (272), he hurriedly leaves New York City to return to Scranton having missed his one chance for social and material advancement in America.

Whereas *Reamer Lou* is a picaresque told in first person narration *The River Between* is a melodrama told in third person narration. Whereas *Reamer Lou* has thirty-five short chapters *The River Between* has three sections: Book I (eighteen short chapters), "Interlude: Ntoni" (which returns to the island Vulcan and events that took place in the past), and Book Two (sixteen short chapters). *The River Between*, in addition, has the complexity of three main characters: Orestes, Rose, and Demetrio—rather than a single organizing consciousness. Whereas Louis's father died when he was very young, Orestes's father is all too present in *The River Between*. Whereas Louis, raised by his Aunt Rosaria, forms a family of sorts with his multi-ethnic co-workers, Orestes's dysfunctional and incestuous extended Italian American family suffocates its members.

Just before the climax of the earlier novel, Louis says that immigrants need "a right path [...] pointed out to them" because when they arrive "they know little. They are in a strange land. They easily make mistakes" (258). Yet, Louis adds, "gradually these immigrant groups blend into America" (258). Of course, the events that follow and that conclude the novel emphatically contradict this claim. And so it is in *The River Between*.

Demetrio, the patriarch of the Lyba family, comes to America because of the mess he made of his life in Italy. As in *Reamer Lou*, friendship and its betrayal is a theme in *The River Between*. Demetrio betrays his friend Maello, fathers a child named Serafina and kills Ntoni, the husband of this child's mother. Demetrio leaves his son with his deceased wife's family on the north coast of Sicily, tries to put an ocean between himself and his reckless past, and over the course of years builds a successful construction company on the New Jersey side of the

Hudson, just across the river from Manhattan. The promise of America fails Demetrio, however, and the misdeeds of his early years follow him, he cannot escape them. He builds a large tenement that at times in the novel sounds positively gothic, on the highland above the Hudson, "perched on the edge of the Palisades" (6). Serafina lives here with her husband Renato. Orestes, after not having seen his father for many years, now lives in this building, too. Eight years before the main events of the novel, Demetrio summoned Orestes to rescue his company. Demetrio deeds his company and house to his son in order to survive a threatened lawsuit. Both fifty-five year old Demetrio and thirty-year old Orestes are men of large build and Herculean physical strength, but the father is going blind and the son is week-willed. Orestes has taken a wife, Rose. Demetrio finds himself attracted to Rose, and Orestes becomes attracted to Serafina. He doesn't know that she is his half-sister, but she suspects that this is so. He doesn't know that his father is attracted to Rose, but Rose senses that this is so. In the house there are also boarders, Italian immigrant laborers. These men, including Renato, work for Orestes's construction company and observe the strange events of this claustrophobic household. In fact, three of the women of the tenement act as a Greek chorus at several points in the novel and even Maello turns up, now an impoverished fruit vendor asking for shelter.

If anything, *The River Between* is even bitterer and angrier than *Reamer Lou*. Four more years of immigration restriction and prejudice against non-white and non-native born peoples could not be offset by Forgione's somewhat successful writing career or his steady work as a naval draughtsman. Was it the Depression that ended his promising literary career or after two successful publications in 1928 did he become frustrated that an author can criticize America so severely precisely because no one listens?

Louis Podesta is the child of immigrants. Demetrio Lyba is an Italian-born immigrant. Louis believes that the immigrants are good, honest people who are corrupted by America. Demetrio comes to America already corrupted, but hoping for both escape and rescue. America, however, as Forgione depicts it, is not innocent. It does not offer asylum. And so when new world corruption meets old world corruption it leads to destruction. The novel ends with the Lyba tenement building in flames.

Demetrio tells his son, "'Never did I think that I would lose everything, my life, my soul, my happiness, piece by piece, bit by bit—like this business, this house, this power which I have lost to you...'" (24). He adds, "'I fled to this country, half way around the world. I worked hard. I built this business. I drove my men like dogs.... And now. I am nothing'" (25). Demetrio's anger grows throughout the first section. His arguments with his son increase and eventually he leaves their home on the Palisades and disappears into the metropolis across the river.

Demetrio attempted to escape his past by fleeing to America, a land, he had heard, of rebirth and opportunity. His son Orestes tried to escape his present, a present in which he runs a successful construction business but is unhappily married, fights constantly with his father, and distinctly cannot fulfill his dreams. He has two dreams: one would send him far away from New Jersey; the other binds him to its shore. Forgione writes early in the novel, "And here he was, stranded on the Palisades, in the haunting presence of a bright metropolis, out of his element, irresolute, deadened, the weight of a big business on his shoulders" (15). What was his unfulfilled ambition? "'Nothing much,'" Orestes tells Serafina, "'simply to be master of a ship, to sail about from port to port, bringing cargoes out of strange shores: wines, silks, rosewoods, crates, bales ... and to be free of this filthy land'" (236). It is his attraction to Serafina, as well as his lack of will and his sense of duty to do, as he repeats often in the novel, the right thing, that keeps him here. Serafina, however, is married to Renato, and so this illicit attraction apparent to all leads first to joking amongst the workers and boarders and quickly to heightened anger and violent fighting between Orestes and Renato. There is no escape for Orestes, just as there isn't any for Demetrio.

Soon after Demetrio leaves the New Jersey homestead, Rose leaves. She, too, seeks escape. Without Demetrio threateningly wandering the corridors of the Lyba tenement, there is nothing to hold Rose and Orestes together. It was the fact that they shared a common enemy that kept them together. Rose feared Demetrio, but she feared him, in part, because she knew that he was attracted to her and that she might be attracted to him. Furthermore, she felt bored with her hardworking husband who went to bed punctually every night at nine. Eventually she feels that Orestes's "very virtues represented everything she hated!" (138). And all the time while in New Jersey high up on the Palisades overlooking the city she thinks, "Imagine! At nine, when the lively world across the river, the world she knew, was just gathering in full swing! The shows were on; the dances were beginning, the jazz, the talk, the fun … what a whirl of joy under the white tents of the city!" (114). While she sees New Jersey as "a confusion of factories, shops, refineries, twined with gleaming railroad tracks," she sees New York City as "beautiful" and as "a metropolis of dreams" (130).

But her Broadway dream, "down around Chatham Square," turns into "the open thresholds of Hell" (196). There is no escape, no success for Rose. She renews her affair with Arthur Halstead and follows him away from her ethnic enclave into a nouveau riche neighborhood on Riverside Drive. Forgione describes the buildings of this neighborhood as "high cliffs of imposing sham" which "betray the inhabitants" airs and presumptions (178). Rose lives the high life for a time with Arthur, "America's Viking Composer" (179), but eventually she moves on to another lover and then begins a precipitous decline.

One day she looks west across the river at the Lyba house "catching the first rose-tint of dawn, blooming with warm color as the clouds opened," and she thinks, "how serene, how peaceful it all appeared! What a picture of simple happiness […]" (188). Yes, the grass on the other side always appears greener (or the lights on the other side always appear brighter). "'God! God!' she exclaimed," Forgione writes, "'Is there always a river between? Always something to separate us from an ideal? Always something to stand between us and an unattainable dream?'" (189-190). As Hendin writes in *The Right Thing to Do* describing the Triborough Bridge from Queens looking toward Manhattan, "If it seemed like a route to possibility, it also implied that some possibilities were out of reach" (31), and so the bright lights of Manhattan are for Rose: promises of endless possibility, but also beams of a blinding glare. After a year in Manhattan she had become "a lost woman." She says, "'I'm a bum. I've been broken in every way that it's possible for a woman to be: I'm a souse. ... I take dope. ...'" (223).

Rose says these words of self-condemnation to Demetrio with whom by chance she has become reacquainted after the police chased her one day. Demetrio, too, has declined. He is now completely blind and Rose decides to help him. She comes to the decision that they can't continue any longer to eke out their deplorable existence in New York and she convinces him to return to Orestes and the house in New Jersey. The river, Forgione says, is "the one reality between two banks of illusion" (252).

In *The Right Thing to Do* the East River below the Triborough Bridge forms a boundary for Gina whereas for Gina's angry father the Atlantic Ocean is the boundary between the old ways of Sicily and the new ways of New York. Though he has crossed this wide boundary, he insists on maintaining the old ways in a new space. It doesn't work and space in this novel, as in *The River Between*, becomes constricting, choking. In their dark, narrow apartment, he rages against his wife, he locks his daughter in her bedroom, and he dies. It is tomb-like, indeed. Hendin describes it as "catacombs for the living dead" (101). They could have bought a house. They could have reached that Italian American property-owning dream as the Angeluzzi-Corbo family does at the end of *The Fortunate Pilgrim*, but Nino believes, as his father used to say, "'When you leave the old ways, you know what you will lose, but not what you'll find'" (25). Yet change is all around Nino in New York: old neighborhoods decline, parks are turned, as he says, "'into slums and cemeteries'" (87), a beloved sister dies, and a daughter grows up. He believes that "since anything could happen, it was better that nothing did" and since things do happen, "he was given to sulking depressions from which anything could erupt" (47).

Anna Giardino's father attempts to adapt to change. Whereas clinging to the old ways failed Nino, attempts at adaptation fail Michello. Like Nino, however, in America Michello becomes very angry. In Italy, Anna recalls in her thoughts, he sang "like an angel," played "all musical instruments," and read books (4). In America this once handsome man became, Anna recalls, "pale under coal dust, dark, with an angry face, angry even when it smiles" (5). Anna thinks, "I don't believe what Mama and the others say about the Old Country, about how he sang and was happy. I don't believe in that man. I only know this one, this cruel, mean man who sleeps in our cabin, this monster [...]" (7). America, Anna realizes, "promised him a new life but instead brings him a new kind of death" (8).

Things get worse. Anna's brother dies in a mine accident. Anna's father becomes more despondent than ever. Then it seems that their luck will change. Mama and Papa buy a farm from a paisano. It seems as if "the dream has come true. But it is only a dream" (11). Michello knows nothing of farming and, bad luck, everything that could possibly go wrong, does. Like Louis Podesta, just as Michello Giardino seems about to attain some modicum of success in America, defeat and despair strike again. Anna thinks to herself, "[...] my father was a slave destroyed by The System [...]" (130). Dorothy Bryant states:

> He had been used and abused by the forces in which he had put all his hope. So had she [Anna]. He had become filled with hatred and bitterness and despair, and had vented his hatred on the nearest targets. So, finally, had she. (146)

The immigrant's anger, an anger often passed on to children, survives far beyond the generation of authors who came of age in the 1930s. In the instance of Louis Forgione, his fiction predates that of Pietro di Donato and John Fante. New York City is the locus, for

Forgione, not of ability, compassion, and tolerance, but of a sham existence, a Madison Avenue lie that can only result in despair followed by rage. One day when Louis and his friend August, the Finn, enter the "cheap sailors' boarding house" where they're staying in Brooklyn, a bum approaches them. "He came," Louis tells us, "with the usual plea that he was starving and needed a dime. I gave him my half-smoked cigarette, and he went on puffing happily toward some other men. I looked in a sort of fear after that bum. Something told me that he had been made that way by this city" (175). Demetrio, too, is made a bum, a beggar by this city. "How the proud and the strong had fallen!" Forgione writes (202). And as this man rendered a "dumb animal," blind and alone, begged, "He heard the howling of men in the night, but sensed nothing of the throbbing silence of their souls. Along the viewless streets surrounding him ran noises and hideous echoes—evil thoughts made audible; the howling of men! The howling of men!" (212).

Chapter 5

ROME, IF YOU WANT

"In the summer of 1960, at the age of fifty-one, John Fante flew from Los Angeles to Rome" (Cooper 3). Thus, Stephen Cooper begins his biography of Fante. The return to ancestral lands has been an important life experience for Italian American writers. So, too, the image of Italy in their work has been important. Italian American author John Fante, born and raised in Colorado and a long-time resident of southern California, occasionally looked east to Italy. His friend Ross B. Wills noted, "John is proud of his Italian background [...] but is not particularly conscious of being Italian" (337). He says that although Fante "has written, thus far [1941], largely about Italian Americans [...] His adult life since 1930, however, has been spent in a general, non-Italian, environment" (337). In his fiction the image of the ancestral land is meaningfully conflicted.

Sociologist Robert Orsi has described how Italian immigrants invented a homeland that never existed and used this invention as a fantasy to assuage their pain and as a stick to discipline their children. So it is in Fante's fiction and letters. In his first published novel, *Wait Until Spring, Bandini* (1938), for example, Arturo Bandini's grandmother disparages the United States and praises the values of a now distant Italy while in the late work *My Dog Stupid* (a novella completed in 1971 and published posthumously in 1986) Italy represents a sanctuary for protagonist Henry Molise, a way out of his current domestic travails, a fantasy to assuage his pain. When Fante finally journeyed to Italy his letters home indicate that he was enthralled and not somewhat disappointed as so many other Italian American authors have been from Jerre Mangione through Helen Barolini to Maria Laurino. Fante's writing changes over time from Italy as strap to Italy as sanctuary, from being driven from the homeland to being drawn to it. This shift demonstrates that the manufactured memories that Orsi described can be appropriated and utilized by the children of immigrants and that these constructions are mutable rather than rigid.

Orsi sets forth his thoughts on Southern Italy as imaginary place and disciplinary tactic in an article published in 1990, "The Fault of Memory: 'Southern Italy' in the Imagination of Immigrants and the Lives of Their Children in Italian Harlem, 1920-1945." In this offshoot study from *The Madonna of 115th Street,* Orsi observes, "'Southern Italy' was always cast as a reproach to the younger generation's emerging sense of the world. With this act of the imagination peculiar to immigrant communities, the immigrants sought to discipline their children with the other place" (136). America was the inverse of Southern Italy, according to Orsi: "money could be made more easily than in 'Southern Italy,' the immigrants conceded, but everything else was wrong" (138). The larger significance of these findings for Orsi is that they demonstrate that "'tradition' is a complex cultural process which does not discover, but creates the past in response to the needs and dilemmas of the present" (133).

In his fiction Fante shaped an image of the past just as Orsi's immigrants of Italian Harlem did; that is, "in response to the needs and dilemmas of the present" (133). As a young author Fante recalls his elders' condemnations of American crassness and praise for Old World ways while his young protagonists often yearn to be "American." When Fante becomes a father who sees his children turning away from him and toward their own path in life, then the products of America become hollow shells for hollow men and a non-mediated life of an idolized homeland becomes the necessary escape.

Fante was not the only Italian American author to explore the contrast between Italy and America, to envision the land of the ancestors as the land of paradise or to describe how nostalgia can be changed into an oftentimes violent discipline. Joseph Papaleo's 1970 novel *Out of Place,* as we'll see at more length in chapter eight, traces the movement of a successful Italian American lawyer as he travels back and forth between southern New York and Southern Italy in search of first his sister's children and then his place in the world. When he arrives in Naples he feels "nostalgia sticking in his throat," but it is not his nostalgia he feels. It is his parents' for "it had been invoked in kitchens until it was both unreal and real, his mother's thoughts and the excuse for her dissatisfactions" (14). Gene Santoro's Italian immigrant brother-in-law, Carlo Marinara, has run-off with the children and Gene has come to Italy to find his sister's son and daughter and bring them back. Carlo asks Gene when they meet in Amalfi, "'Are they children over there, driven to stores, walking through stores? Objects! Did they live? Did they see anything like this? Here something enters you. There, you are hollow'" (36). Eventually, Gene begins to feel that something which enters one in Italy. "The wandering was good," Gene thinks, "washed the mind, removed the film, the cast of sameness from the eye's view, erased the drugstore sandwich of his lunch hours, his desk, the telephone like a wire leash from home to office" (237). Gene decides to let his partner handle the law firm, leave his two sons in private school, get his wife, and move to Italy for good. He tells his wife "'we got the dream; we got Westchester. And I ought to know. I helped build this living cemetery myself. I don't think *any* of us ever liked it here, this dead place with empty streets. And people around here who never liked us—we were too *dark* for them'" (259). His wife argues that she doesn't need to live in Italy to feel a sense of self-worth. Gene wonders, then, why his wife Francine has her hair bleached blond every week. She replies it's just a style, a fashion. "'All right,'" Gene adds, "'then what's in style over there is *me*. Everything likes me there. I match'" (261). Francine, nonetheless, still feels that Italy is a "dream world" and that living there "would be like suspension in air" (262).

An author can paint a fanciful or realistic picture of a presumed Italian paradise. Often, this depends on the author's or a character's generational place. For example, Grandma Doria in Tina De Rosa's *Paper Fish* yearns for Italy where her ill granddaughter Doriana "would run in green fields under the healthy sun, would play in the white sunlight, would reach up and receive from the hands of the sky, from the blessed guardian angels, her own healthy mind" (64). Chicago, on the other hand, she believes, sucked "the blood of the wonderful child [...]" (64). Her son Marco, a policeman, "went out where people were murdered, were butchered like pigs in the sties" (64). If he lived in Italy, according to Grandma Doria, he would "gather olives, sit in the sun" (64).

Louise DeSalvo's place in generational immigrant history corresponds to that of Doria's granddaughters Doriana and Carmalina, and in her memoir *Adultery* DeSalvo tempers her Italian fantasy with a dose of self-restraining realism. Canio, the owner of a bookstore that she frequents, introduces Louise to Fabio "who runs a waterfront restaurant in Italy's Lake District during the summer months, and who spends the rest of his time traveling" (157-158). This handsome man who leads this idyllic life could be her revenge lover for her husband's affair. "*In another time*, in another place, in another life, in another narrative, Fabio and I might have become lovers [...]," she says, but she realizes "that though it might have brought me much pleasure, it surely, too, would have entailed more sorrow that I now am willing to experience" (159).

In addition to Italy as a place of nostalgia or escape, Italian American authors have described it as a strap for disciplining children. No character in all of Italian American literature more desires to beat his offspring with an invented past than Nino Giardello in Josephine Gattuso Hendin's *The Right Thing to Do*. The phrase that forms the title of this book appears at least twenty-two times in it and Southern Italian proverbs abound. Nino tells his wife: "'My father used to say, 'When you leave the old ways, you know what you will lose, but not what you'll find'" (25). Perhaps, Nino's limp and diabetes symbolize the dysfunctional nature of his approach to family relations. He is to the Italian American family as Captain Ahab is to the American whaling industry. In an insightful scene in Washington Square Park, Hendin reveals Nino's and his daughter's view of the Garibaldi statue. The fact that these two people, father and daughter, view the same thing in a different way expresses their antagonism and also their connection. They do, after all, both see the statue in the park, but Nino see "a man," "the kind of man you could see would use his sword to defend the right things" (79) and Gina sees a statue "already flecked and pitted with soot [...]" (80). When Nino catches Gina in a silky orange kimono at her son-of-an-American-historian boyfriend's apartment, he warns her, "'In Sicily you wouldn't be alive'" (92). After this Gina moves out, but her new apartment may be only a transitional space and not a true sanctuary for it is as confining as the space she left. As Hendin writes, "By stretching her arms, she could touch both sides of the room" (110).

When the Italian American author returns to the land of parents, grandparents, great-grandparents' birth does the author find sanctuary or does the author, to borrow and adapt a phrase from Emerson, "carry his giant with him wherever he goes"?[1] Invariably, Rome pleases the Italian American author, but the ancestral village disappoints and the author never finds in that village what he or she had hoped to discover there. What Antonio Mangano said of Southern Italy after his visit there in 1907, other authors repeat up to the present moment. "We frequently saw," Mangano recalls, "human beings and domestic animals living together in miserable straw huts strengthened with mud, indescribably dirty [...]." "In many remote towns," he says, "mediaeval customs still prevail, and the manner of living has not improved for centuries" (17).

At the conclusion of his memoir *Mount Allegro* (1942) Jerre Mangione upon arriving at his mother's hometown observes that, "the only heartening sight was the Mediterranean coming into a wide inlet about a mile away [...]." He notes that, "the nearest water supply was seven

---

[1] The full paragraph of which the borrowed phrase forms the last sentence reads in its entirety: "Travelling is a fool's paradise. Our first journeys discover to us the indifference of places. At home I dream that at Naples, at Rome, I can be intoxicated with beauty and lose my sadness. I pack my trunk, embrace my friends, embark on the sea and at last wake up in Naples, and there beside me is the stern fact, the sad self, unrelenting, identical, that I fled from. I see the Vatican and the palaces. I affect to be intoxicated with sights and suggestions, but I am not intoxicated. My giant goes with me wherever I go" ("Self-Reliance" 198). Travel for Emerson is one of the cultural forces and institutions that deter us from trusting ourselves.

miles away." And so "every morning a man with a mule and a cart brought a barrel of water to Realmonte [...]" (256). Yet, despite the mediaeval customs and conditions Mangione's Uncle Nino dreams of leaving Rochester, New York and returning to Italy someday, a land whose beauty he recalls and whose people's manners he distinctly remembers as far less crass and materialistic than those of his American neighbors. An old family friend who returned to Sicily from America tells the visiting Jerre Mangione to tell his uncle "'to stay where he is. He would not be happy if he came back [...] I wish I had never left America. Things are not as I expected to find them'" (285).

Helen Barolini offers an interesting explanation for why the returning Italian American cannot find what she seeks in the ancestral land. At the end of the chapter in *Umbertina* in which Tina returns to her great-grandparents' hometown of Castagna she comes to understand that "the revelation she had to find was not in the mountains of Calabria, but in her own mind" (393). Tina arrives in Calabria playing a game of identity politics for she sees her ethnic identity as something that is or which should be fixed and essential. But after her journey to the ancestral home and compounded by discoveries made latter at Ellis Island and on Cape Cod, she shifts to a sort of post-ethnic approach to identity. This "new construct," as David Biale has written regarding contemporary American Jewish identity, "would posit that identity [could] be individually chosen. Identity in such a theory is fluid and often multiple" (30).

Granted, Barolini published *Umbertina* well-before the discussion of post-ethnic theory and, as she outlined in an essay originally published in *Italian Americana,* Tina's trip to Castagna follows to some extent the author's own trip there many years prior, the movement from identity politics to post-ethnicity explains the experiences of many Italian American authors who take the trip back not just to the great city, but to the dusty village, too.

Barolini resided in Rome at the time she planned her Castagna trip. Her friends told her "no one *goes* to Calabria [...] it's a place to leave" ("Calabrian Journey" 75). She arrived in Calabria and, she says, "the word *brullo* kept coming to mind: bare, stripped, barren, bleak, desolate, scorched, the color of a *crème brulee*" (76). (She used this exact image in *Umbertina*—describing Tina's reaction to Calabria.) She loses confidence in the purpose of her journey: "to visit a village which I would simply look at and then leave, a tourist of my provenance" (76). When she arrives at Castagna she wonders where all the people are and she is told that they have left. Tina, too, is told the same thing. Tina, too, feels "oppressed" by the "dusty little villages" of Calabria (*Umbertina* 372). Tina wonders, "What had she in common with the impoverished hovels of this place [...] with the isolation and backwardness? She was now a product of education. There was no return" (*Umbertina* 384). There is no return, but through education—life experience as much as book learning, Barolini tells us there may be change and there may be choice.

For example in Barolini's short story "The Nordic Type" a young Italian American is surprised to find Italy "so hard" even though it is "the country of her grandparents" (50). This visitor, Michele, like other Barolini characters is in search of her "'place in the world'" (51). She hopes to find place and purpose in Italy and yet "in fact, her mother's Italian cooking was better than anything she had had in Italy. Was Italy a mistake?" (55). She wonders. Michele visits an eccentric Countess. This is the life-experience that leads her to choice and change. At first, Michele dislikes this woman who near the story's conclusion declares, "'I'm not like most Italians who'll only swim in the luke-warm Adriatic Sea. I'm really a Nordic type, you know'" (58). Michele's opinion of the Countess changes and Michele begins to think: "what type am I?" (58). She concludes that the Countess "knew who she was and though it was an impossible combination (and scarcely a real one), she had made that combination be true, be herself" (58). Whereas before her visit Michele thought she had to become "all of one piece," she now understands that "We are not made of whole cloth; we are shreds and tatters, Harlequins and Columbines, a crazy quilt, *mélange* assorti" (58). In other words, like Tina, Michele has moved from an identity politics sense of self to a self-constructed post-ethnic approach to self. This new sense of self enables her to feel more comfortable in Italy, too, for she has now cast off her giant.

The essays in Maria Laurino's bestseller, *Were You Always an Italian?*, also trace a similar pattern of self-understanding. Her first essay, "Scents," describes her childhood sense of ethnic shame, an important theme in Fante's work. As an adult she comes to love Italy and things Italian. Periodically she lives in Rome, but like many other Italian American authors it takes her quite sometime to journey from the great city to the dusty village. In her writing she connects her trip to the ancestral home with the death of a grandparent. She writes: "My grandfather insisted that he would one day return to southern Italy to retire, but he died years before his dream could take place. No one from my immediate family had ever seen the town of Conza della Campania until I traveled there in 1996 [...]" (14). Like other Italian American authors, Laurino, who loves Rome, feels remorse and guilt that she was slow to journey south and when she first gets there, dislikes it. "I didn't want to admit," she writes, "that in nearly fifteen years of coming to Italy I had made just one disastrous attempt to travel south with my brother during our first trip: we arrived in Naples, and I was so overcome by its chaos and poverty that I insisted we take the next train back to Rome" (92-92). She confesses, "I had embraced the Italy of the north, a world away from my roots [...]" (94).[2]

---

[2] In a 2001 essay on Carole Maso, Roseanne Giannini Quinn has written: "What constitutes *Italian-American* culture for a third-generation daughter born of a second-generation parent? Like many of my generation, I searched for answers to that question by traveling to Italy to the places I thought of as my homeland. [...] I did not visit my grandparents' place of birth, Lucca and Sestri Levanti, where I still have many family members. I went instead to Venice and Verona and Rome. I saw the Spanish Steps and had tea at Keats's house and spoke sporadic Italian. But I saw myself there somehow. [...] At the same time I know that Italy is not my home." As for me, the places of the Southern Italian past do appear in what I write. I have visited them only once (but want to return). I, too, love Rome, but I love Naples, too. I'm not sure how much time I should spend in the ancestral towns of the South. For it may be easier to write of an imagined place than of an actual one.

When she finally takes her trip south she, too, compares the ancestral home to something primitive and forsaken: "Nuova Conza reminded me of a Potemkin. Most of the residents can't afford to pay for electricity [...]" (195). Her cousin Franco shows her around. She recalls in language similar to that Mangano used in 1908, "we followed a steep, curving passageway back to the Middle Ages. Within the walled villages, women all in black balanced firewood on their heads as they walked, and donkeys were used to transport goods" (196). What she learns from this trip resembles what Tina learned from her trip south, what Michele learned from her visit with the Countess. Laurino notes:

> I could say that my family traces its roots to Dante Alighieri, a ridiculous lie. Or I could say that I was at home arriving in Rome because of my Italian roots, which is not an out-and-out lie but a skewed interpretation of facts based on my wants at the time [...] Rome is a world away from the poverty and isolation of southern Italy. Or I could argue that some of my personality traits are linked to a peasant ancestry, which again is a stretch of the imagination, another form of gamesmanship. (202)

Laurino has learned through life experience Orsi's thesis regarding tradition; that is, "the articulation of a 'tradition' is a complex cultural process which does not discover, but creates the past in response to the needs and dilemmas of the present" ("The Fault of Memory" 133).

Fante, too, created his traditions out of his current needs. Cooper records that when Fante went to Torricella Peligna in the fall of 1960, "His father's hometown struck him as a wretched and unlivable place, at once familiar and as foreign as a bad dream" (*Full of Life* 7-8). Yet, after an earlier trip to Italy Fante wrote his friend Carey McWilliams, "I was in Italy last summer for 7 weeks, in Naples mostly, but some days in Rome, on a movie project. It was a very moving and important experience for me" (*Selected Letters* 260).

Indeed, Fante, like the protagonist of Papaleo's *Out of Place*, considers moving his family to Italy. While he realizes that this would be impractical if not impossible, he does see Italy in a manner similar to the characters Gene and Carlo in *Out of Place*. Fante, too, feels that Italy fills a void that America cannot fill. Fante begins one letter to his wife: "Living in America, we tend to think other places lack style, modernity, and that our way of life is the best in the world. Don't you believe it" (*Selected Letters* 247). In Naples, he effuses to Joyce; the laundry is cleaner than in Los Angeles, "the courtesy is amazing," and "the pasta is from heaven [...]" (*Selected Letters* 247). Even though, he admits, there are sharp class divisions, the rich and the poor in Italy, he says, "love each other, they regard each other with gallantry and respect" (*Selected Letters* 248). Two days later he writes to Joyce, "I don't care how big California fruits grow, here they're bigger" (*Selected Letters* 251). One void that Italy can fill and fill well is an empty stomach! Yet, only nine days later he tells his wife, "The luster of Naples had to wear off, and it has" (257). And yet in his more self-reflective letter to Carey McWilliams it is aspects of the sweet life, *la dolce vita*, of the film industry that he finds wanting whereas the people of Italy, he says, are "simply gorgeous, courteous, and refined. Even the lowest peasant in Italy," he adds, "is somehow born to a culture and degree of civilized living that we don't know" (*Selected Letters* 260).

It is no wonder that Fante's trips to Italy in the late fifties, early sixties would be significant to him for he had been thinking about Italy and things Italian his entire life. It is also no wonder that he should have some contrasting feelings about his ancestral land for in his life in Southern California and in his literary writings he presented what Stefano Luconi has called a "protean ethnicity."

In 1933 he tells his cousin, "I want to cover the true Italian-American scene, as yet pretty much untouched" (*Selected Letters* 39). This same year he tells his mentor H. L. Mencken, "I am innately an Italian whom other Italians take immediate dislike to. I feel that I should exploit this capacity I have for making Italians hate me" (*Fante / Mencken* 60). The year prior Mencken had warned Fante, "I have a feeling that you had better stop writing about your family. The subject seems to obsess you" (*Fante / Mencken* 37). After the failure to secure publication for

The Road to Los Angeles (finished in 1936), Fante returned to the strictly Italian America subject matter that had brought him success with his early short story publications and wrote *Wait Until Spring, Bandini* which became in 1938 his first published novel even though it was the second one he completed. In 1940 Fante complains in his diary, "Publishers discourage me. They always want what I don't feel like doing. Phillips [Frances Phillips of Morrow] was only faintly interested in the Filipino book. She wants a big Italian book from me" (324). His editor at Viking, Pascal Covici, on the other hand, encouraged Fante to attempt his "Little Brown Brothers" book as Fante had thought to call his Filipino novel that he abandoned and then picked up and abandoned again.

At this time Fante co-authored with Ross B. Wills an original story called "Mama Ravioli" which became the 1940 film *East of the River*. Fante had never been East and while it is difficult to say with precision what aspects of the narrative originated with Fante, it is nonetheless interesting to note that in this film New York, or at least Mama's restaurant and embrace, offers sanctuary from the corruption of West Coast crime.[3]

Although it took him a long time to travel to Italy, the aspiration to go there was a long-held one. In 1934 he told his mother that he planned to apply for a Guggenheim so that he could spend "a year in Italy, with six months in Rome, and six months in Naples. Or better still," he said, "I may ask for a full 12 months in Abruzzi, where Papa's people come from" (*Selected Letters* 71).

Fante's aspirations and social reality sometimes clashed. Not only did he get turned down when he applied for a Guggenheim, but during the war while doing work for the Office of War Information he had hoped to go "to New York and write some feature for OWI to be beamed at

---

[3] *East of the River* offers an interesting reversal of the commonplace American cultural theme of *translatio studii*—civilization ever moves westward and is always corrupted by the east. Sklar does not discuss this film in *City Boys*. It is an entertaining Garfield vehicle and the urban locus of the story fits Sklar's topic.

Italy" (*Selected Letters* 197) or to go to North Africa and "instruct the Italians in the occupied territory on American democratic principles" (*Selected Letters* 201). Fante failed, however, to gain sufficient proficiency in Italian to undertake either of these tasks.

Rudolph J. Vecoli has said that what it means to be Italian American "varies according to geography, gender, social class, and political disposition" (313). I would add that what it means to be Italian American also varies for each individual at various times in their lives and that Fante's fiction demonstrates this. In his early fiction parental figures oftentimes condemn America and use an imaginary Italy as a means to discipline children. In later fiction (most notably *My Dog Stupid*) the protagonist is now a middle-aged adult and a parent and dreams of an escape to Italy.

In Fante's first published novel, *Wait Until Spring, Bandini* (1938), his protagonist, the young Arturo Bandini, yearns to forsake his ethnicity and be what he conceptualizes as a full-fledged "American." Fante writes:

> His name was Arturo, but he hated it and wanted to be called John. His last name was Bandini, and he wanted it to be Jones. His mother and father were Italians, but he wanted to be an American. His father was a bricklayer, but he wanted to be a pitcher for the Chicago Cubs. (33)

Svevo Bandini, Arturo's father, is proud that he is a naturalized American citizen (216), but he is also proud of his Italian birth: "no people on earth equaled the Italian people" (202) he thinks at one point even though when quizzed about Italian high culture by Effie Hildegarde he admits ignorance of that Italy. With his Italy he sometimes disciplines his sons:

> "When I was a boy," Bandini began. "When I was a boy back in the Old Country –"
> At once Federico and Arturo left the table. This was old stuff to them. They knew he was going to tell them for the ten thousandth time that he made four cents a day carrying stone on his back, when he was a boy, back

> in the Old Country, carrying stone on his back, when he was a boy. The story hypnotized Svevo Bandini. It was dream stuff that suffocated and blurred Helmer the banker, holes in his shoes, a house not paid for, and children that must be fed. When I was a boy: dream stuff. (40-41)

In other words, this repeated reminiscence is more than a reproach for the boys' laziness. It is, like those nostalgic tales told by immigrants of Italian Harlem, a fantasy used to assuage the immigrant's, Svevo Bandini's, pain and disappointment. Looking back to Italy is another way to negotiate America.

Svevo's mother-in-law, on the other hand, shows no mixed feeling for America, but only condemns it. Whenever she comes to visit, Svevo leaves the house, goes off on a binge, and doesn't return until she is gone. When Donna Toscana arrives and inspects the house and takes note of Svevo's absence and Maria's, her daughter and Svevo's wife, lack of authority she bemoans, "'Ah, America! Only in this corrupt land could such things happen'" (93). At dinner that night she complains that "'the dinner is badly prepared'" and that the "'spaghetti tastes like dung'" (94). Only in America, Donna Toscana feels, could a daughter be such a disappointment to her mother.

In 1940 when Fante wavered between a Filipino project and an Italian one he began a novel called "Ah, Poor America." His introductory letter and sample pages that he sent to Pascal Covici survive. He told his Viking Press editor, "I'm going to write a book with humor in it as well as tragedy. For tragedy it will be, as a whole: tragedy of a man who let his dreams slip through his fingers" (*Selected Letters* 179). The pages he enclosed he said were "rough, of course, but swell too" (*Selected Letters* 176). One character in the "swell" book-to-have-been is the mother/wife, Donna Scarpi, who in the sample excerpt fumes in the kitchen.

> Donna Scarpi was angry with the peas. She hated the grocer who sold them, because he was an American, and she hated the store because it was in Denver, which was in America, and she hated America because it was not Italy. (*Selected Letters* 178)

A decade later Fante includes a character similar to Donna Toscana and Donna Scarpi in his novel *1933 Was a Bad Year*. Fante began this novel right after *Full of Life*, but he put it aside in 1954 and completed it later. In it Grandma Bettina complaints that she "'traveled five thousand miles in steerage to a barbarian land'" (17) and she asks to be sent back to her hometown, Torricella Peligna. Young Dominic Molise knows why she feels this way.

> There had been poverty in Abruzzi too, but it was a sweeter poverty that everyone shared like bread passed around. Death was shared too, and grief, and good times, and the village of Torricella Peligna was like a single human being. My grandmother was a finger torn from the rest of the body and nothing in the new life could assuage her desolation. (18)

The communal ways of the Old World contrast with the New World cult of the individual. Dominic would assert himself through the force of his pitching talent. Yet, this ego assertion also leads to "desolation" and a severing. Dominic constantly refers to his pitching arm as "The Arm"; thus, showing how he has become alienated from himself, from his very own body.

When Dominic steals his father's cement mixer so that he can raise money for a quixotic trip to California and a tryout with the Cubs, Grandma Bettina catches him and asks Dominic not to do it. She says, "'So this is the American way'" (112). Dominic begins to feel overwhelmed by guilt as he drives near his grandfather's grave. "The lure of fame and fortune," he narrates, "had turned me into a madman. Was this to be Grandpa's reward for coming all the way from Abruzzi, so that his grandson should blight his grave with stolen goods?" (115).

A much more humorous reference to Old World ancestors occurs in Fante's prior full-length fiction of the 1950s, *Full of Life* (1952). Here the reference isn't used to chastise a younger generation as much as to instill a sense of pride. "John Fante," the protagonist in this novel, must type his father "Nick's" story of Uncle Mingo so that it can be passed on to the child to whom the character "Joyce Fante" is soon to give birth. It is true that Nick uses this narrative to manipulate his son, but there's no bitterness here. This story of Uncle Mingo is more slapstick than disciplinary strap. As Nick narrates he drinks more and more and his tale of Uncle Mingo and the bandits becomes disjointed, full of absurd non sequitur. It is a brilliant passage. John stays with his Dad until his father dozes off from two bottles of Chianti, some Martell and Galliano. Nick wanders from one detail to another but never gets to the bandits. After Nick falls asleep and John helps him to his room, John stays up until four in the morning typing Uncle Mingo and the bandits, twenty pages. Later that morning with pride he tosses the manuscript to his father who says, "'Save it for the boy.'" John asks, "'Don't you want to read it?'" And Nick replies, "What I got to read it for? Good God, kid, I lived it'" (97). And so in this novel where the main character is about to become a father instead of being a young boy or young man, Fante provides a humorous variation on parents or grandparents using Old World narrative to discipline New World children.

In two works from the thirties in which the protagonist is a young man there are strong proclamations of American identity. In *The Road to Los Angeles* (finished in 1936, but published in 1985), Arturo Bandini announces, "'I'm a writer, man! An American writer, man! [...] I was born right here in the good old U.S.A. under the stars and stripes'" (66). Similarly, in *Ask the Dust* (1939) Arturo states, "I was an American, and god-damn proud of it. This great city [Los Angeles], these mighty pavements and proud buildings, they were the voice of my America. From sand and cactus we Americans had carved an empire" (44). And yet in his last fiction, *Dreams from Bunker Hill*, a novel that looks back to Arturo Bandini's early days in Los Angeles but that, nonetheless, is also the author's last word, Fante/Bandini says the following about Los Angeles and its relation to his self-identity:

> What am I doing here, I asked. I hate this place, this friendless city. Why was it always thrusting me away like an unwanted orphan? Had I not paid my dues? Had I not worked hard, tried hard? What did it have against me?

> Was it the incessant sense of my peasantry, the old conviction that somehow I did not belong? (132)

And if he did not belong even after playing the game for so long and according to the strict rules, then where did he belong? Would he, like Gene Santoro in Papaleo's *Out of Place*, fit or imagine a fit somewhere in Italy, maybe not in Torricella Peligna but in Naples or Rome?

In his late novella *My Dog Stupid* (completed in 1971) protagonist Henry Molise looks to the ancestral homeland for escape and sanctuary, if not rescue, from his mid-life problems of troubling children and dissatisfying work. Near the start of the novella Henry describes his residence with a self-mocking tone: "the entire layout," he says, "looked exactly like what it was not—the domicile of a successful writer" (11). To alleviate his mounting sense of failure he thinks of "grabbing an Al Italia for Rome with seventy thousand bucks in my jeans and a new life in the Piazza Navonne [...]" (11).

Besides family and financial problems, Henry has difficulty with his writing. He tells us that he constantly begins various projects, but abandons them "for lack of confidence and discipline" (55). Now, however, he has fifteen thousand words toward a new novel. Not bad. But he begins to think that he must be alone to complete it and starts, once more, to daydream of Rome. He'd have to get "the kids off our backs" and sell the house, he thinks (55). At this point in his thoughts, he plans to take Harriet, his wife, with him—just like Gene Santoro in *Out of Place*. He considers: "With the kids gone and the house sold I would be loaded, and free" (55). But, Henry says, "The more I planned and dreamed, the less Harriet figured in the project. I don't think she would care for Rome after all" (55).

The disappointments for Henry mount in the story, although they are usually humorous and narrated in a self-mocking tone. For example, Henry checks out some work on a TV series called "Lucky Pierre." As Henry says, "the hero was a dog, a fucking little French poodle named Pierre [...]" (49). Henry hates little dogs and has befriended a lost Akita because, as Henry succinctly puts it, "He was a misfit and I was a misfit"

(43). An old friend of Henry's, Joe Crispi, is in charge of this TV production. Joe, Henry recalls, "had come out of the coal fields of Pennsylvania, published a novel that dealt with the poverty and despair of Italian miners [...]" (48), but now Joe oversees "fawning writers" about to set to work on the "wretched" "Lucky Pierre" (49). Henry, once again, feels that he is a misfit. On the other hand, home does not offer much solace from the cruel cold shoulder of a troubling world. Soon after this dismal afternoon at the studio, his son Denny says, "'Dad, you're a lousy writer'" and then proceeds to explain why (70).

Henry doesn't sell the house, but he does sell some of his prized possessions and plans to sell the single most valuable object he owns—another illusory symbol of the would-be successful Southern Californian writer—his Porsche. He figures, "If I could get eight hundred for my equity [from the foreign car dealer] I'd have close to fifteen hundred for the trip. Subtracting the fare, I'd touch down in Rome with around nine hundred. I could live three months on that" (131). He takes the bus to Point Dume and calls his wife for a ride back to their house. Harriet asks him, where is his car. Henry says he sold it. She asks why and he replies, "'Because I'm leaving for Rome, remember? Checking out. Leaving the country. Back to my origins, back to the cradle of civilization, back to the meaning of meaning, the alpha and omega. Goodbye to Point Dume, to kids and dogs and a wife who never understood me and never will'" (133). She hangs up. He walks home from the bus stop, one mile. He doesn't go to Rome.

He realizes, much like Dominic Molise at the end of *1933 Was a Bad Year*, that he "had painted" himself "into a corner with wild threats" (133). Now he had to go through with them even though thoughts of "cold marble hotel floors sent a chill through" his "feet" (133) and he'd "miss the World Series" (134). If family relations are one of the factors that propelled his desire for escape, then those very same relations are also the main impetus for him to stay.

Stupid, the misfit Akita, has gotten lost. The man who finds Stupid calls Henry asking for a large reward. Harriet tells him not to pay it.

Henry says he promised their son Jamie that nothing would happen to Stupid. Harriet tells Henry he can't afford to pay this ransom. Henry says yes he can and throws his wallet, thick with money, on the table. "'But your trip to Rome!'" Harriet exclaims. And Henry, who is secretly glad that he has a face-saving means to get out of fulfilling his threats to leave, says, "'What's Rome if you have to live with the betrayal of your own son? [...] My duty is clear. God knows I have my faults, but I won't stand accused of disloyalty to my children'" (135). And so there will be no running away, no escape to Rome.

But Fante adds an exclamation point. In the final two chapters Henry both adds to the family that he would have abandoned and his children, in a sense, abandon him. When Henry goes for Stupid he discovers that his Akita has become fond of and attached to a pig named Emma and so Henry returns to exclusive Point Dume not only with his misfit dog, but with an eccentric pig, too. In the final chapter Henry describes the corral he's adapted for Stupid and Emma and then he looks around his Y-shaped ranch at Point Dume and recalls small details associated with each of his children. He realizes that they are all grown and gone now. Thus, he has gotten one of the things he so desired and then he begins to cry (143).

"The history of the Italian American family is the history of conflict," Robert Orsi states in "The Fault of memory" (143). "Dysfunction, pain, and alienation," he asserts, "[...] were as much, if not more, a part of the history of immigrant families as mutual support and group cooperation" (143). Therefore, he believes, it is essential that scholars place "conflict at the center of our understanding of Italian American family history" (142). I would add that it is hard to read Italian American fiction and not see this conflict. For in this body of literature conflict and coercion are ever-present.

John Fante's fiction, with its blurring of the boundary between author and protagonist, provides an important point of origin in a truthful recounting of our Italian American past. His references to Italy as strap or sanctuary form an important and meaningful motif in his work.

This motif is important and meaningful because it shows change over time, and thus the ever-evolving process of ethnic identification, and because he never sought to be a celebrant for the orthodoxy of immigrant boosters who proclaimed success through cooperation. He told it, instead, as he saw it and lived it and although this may have rendered his work more truthful it may also have kept him an outsider, a misfit as much as his dog Stupid.

Chapter 6

BEATING THE MARBLES GAME

According to his friend and fellow writer Ross B. Wills (337), John Fante served as the model for the minor character Willie in William Saroyan's play *The Time of Your Life*. Willie is "a marble-game [pinball] maniac" (23). He plays pinball in the background throughout most of the play. He has few lines. Near the end of the play he beats the pinball machine. He says, "Took me awhile, but I finally did it. It's scientific really. With a little skill a man can make a modest living beating the marble-games. Not that that's what I want to do" (105). More than twenty-five years after his death has Fante begun to beat the pinball game of literary reputation? Is this what he wanted to do or did he want to play pinball, golf, gamble, carouse, and spend money faster than he earned it? Has good marketing moved him from outsider status to celebrant of a posthumous success?

Fante scholar Stephen Cooper published an edited volume entitled *The John Fante Reader*. The book jacket copy calls Fante "a voice of his generation" and an "irrepressible genius" and yet this collection is "the important next step in the reintroduction of this influential writer [...]". It seems somewhat odd "that a writer, almost unheard of in his lifetime" could also be an "irrepressible" and "influential" "voice." The jacket copy concludes by claiming that Fante "is finally taking his place in the pantheon of twentieth-century American writers." Does a literary artist climb Parnassus only with a mighty heave from the biceps of marketing? If so, is the marketing of an author different from or a betrayal of "genius" ("irrepressible" or other wise)? Is it cheating, then: tilting the machine without getting caught so that the author's flag will rise over the terra-formed terrain of the reading public's imagination?

For example, Cooper in his biography of Fante says that this author whose work "would even come to be compared favorably to masterpieces of world literature written by the likes of Knut Hamsum and Dostoevsky" (8), "whatever genius he might possess would have to be put on hold for a time, while Fante attended to the business at hand" (117)—film-script writing. Here we see that Cooper perpetuates the legends of literature and film. Novels are potential "masterpieces" while films are "business." Must filmmaking be rendered villainous so that one screenwriter's novels can be elevated? Is this how Fante scholars tilt the machine in their subject's favor?

Richard Collins in his "literary portrait" of John Fante paints the film industry as any author's Armageddon. "Looking back on his time in Hollywood," Collins writes,

> Fante may well have regarded it as a waste of time and a corruption of his career as a serious writer. But in the early years he welcomed the advantages Hollywood offered: the easy money, the proximity to stardom, the drinking bouts, and the chance to meet other writers succumbing to the same temptations. (164)

For Fante boosters Hollywood is a devil in disguise. Look how quickly in Collins's writing "advantages" become "temptations."

Catherine J. Kordich compliments Fante's screenwriting in her book. Yet, Fante's own friend, Ross Wills, described Fante's career in Hollywood as "a professional flop" (334). While some might recall *Walk on the Wild Side* for which Fante shared a credit with Edmund Morris or enjoy Fante's film version of his own novel *Full of Life*, few will have seen and if seen will remember such films as *The Golden Fleecing*.

In a review essay of Cooper's Fante biography Neil Gordon considers the question "did Hollywood strangle his [Fante's] talent, or did he do it himself?" The title of Gordon's essay, "Shanghaied in Tinseltown," reveals a bias. Gordon links screenwriting with gambling and drinking as if it is an addiction, a sickness rather than a profession or an art: "A heroic drinker and a driven gambler, consumed by dreams of fame and ever hungry for money, Fante seems determined to dive into the exploitative depths of B-movie projects rather than pursuing the critical reputation that was, literally, within his reach."

In his letters Fante himself frequently blamed Hollywood for his problems as a writer of fiction. Yet, in his fiction his alter egos blame themselves. Oddly, then, his fiction offers a truer image of his Hollywood experience and its effect on his efforts to write literary fiction than does his correspondence. Whereas Fante both perpetuates and complicates the legend of the writer in Hollywood, Fante scholars unquestioningly perpetuate it in order to elevate their subject.

"From the start," according to Cooper, "Fante's attitude toward Hollywood was utilitarian and cynical" (111). But from where did Fante's attitude come, if he had it "from the start"? An industry that destroys writers and writers who view the art-destroying industry cynically are characteristics of the writer-in-Hollywood legend. At the same time that "his deeper emotional investments were reserved for the novel [...]," according to Cooper, Fante and Wills "were concocting 'a nasty piece of hypocrisy' in the form of a scenario about the murder of John Dillinger [...]" (112). In Fitzgerald's unfinished Hollywood novel *The Last Tycoon*, the protagonist, Monroe Stahr, a producer, tries to explain some basics about scriptwriting to Boxley, an English writer that Stahr has brought to his studio. Boxley tells Stahr, "'I don't think you people read things. The men are dueling when the conversation takes place. At the end one of them falls into a well and has to be hauled up in a bucket.'" Stahr replies, "'Would you write that in a book of your own, Mr. Boxley?'" And Boxley says, "'What? Naturally not.'" "'You'd consider it too cheap,'" Stahr adds. Boxley says that movie standards differ from book standards and, besides, he never goes to them. "'Isn't it because people are always dueling and falling down wells?'" Stahr asks (31-32). Fante resembles Boxley, except that whereas Boxley quickly learns a thing or two about script construction, Fante was, at best, a slow-learner. Fante stubbornly adhered to characteristic beliefs of the writer-in-

Hollywood legend, beliefs that he brought with him to Hollywood and found reinforcement for once employed in the film industry.

Richard Fine has described the writer-in-Hollywood legend in his book *Hollywood and the Profession of Authorship, 1928-1940*. In "the Hollywood-as-destroyer legend," according to Fine, "[..] the film industry itself was the true villain of the tale" (3). Although Fine's study concludes in 1940, the legend continued well beyond that year. Indeed, it is alive and thriving in the present. John Gregory Dunne's memoir about his co-authorship with his wife, Joan Didion, of the script for *Up Close and Personal* bears the title *Monster*. The industry is the monster destroying Dunne and Didion with hotel suites in Hawaii and lunches in New York at Fifth Avenue's Hotel Pierre. Dunne never once in the memoir mentions how much he and Didion received for their work. It would have been rhetorically unwise to do so. The purpose of Fine's work, however, is not to perpetuate the legend, but to analyze it. He notes that the "legend does not always hold true: too many writers enjoyed successful and productive careers in the film industry [...]" (10).

The most important observation that Fine makes is the following: "the studios defined what a 'writer' was and did far differently—so differently in Hollywood, in fact, that it presented a serious challenge to writers' conceptions of themselves as 'writers' in the Eastern sense" (41). The successful writer James M. Cain in a 1933 *American Mercury* essay said that for the writer-in-Hollywood "his best, if you are to believe him, is the one thing the movies won't let him do" (138). Fante believed it. Cain did not. Fante read, admired, and contributed to *The American Mercury* in which George Jean Nathan, H. L. Mencken's co-editor, often disparaged the film industry. In a 1940 letter Mencken even told Fante, "I never listen to the radio" (*Fante / Mencken* 129). Fante, on the other hand, wrote to Mencken, "*The American Mercury* has been my birth place, my home, my school, my sweetheart, my playground" (*Fante / Mencken* 54). While Fante learned well some of his lessons, his "Eastern" elitist ones, he seems never to have learned the Boxley lesson, and, therefore, Fante proposed ideas for movies that he never would have proposed for novels. Cain said "that the studios don't want good work from a writer, but only the cheapest stuff he can think up [...] is their [the writers'] most frequent out, what they blame their troubles on. Well, I don't believe it" (140). Fante did believe it. At least, his letters indicate that this is so, but his screenwriting alter egos, Arturo Bandini and Henry J. Molise, complicate the issue.

Screenwriter Philip Dunne, who worked in the film industry during the same years as Fante and who knew him but was not part of his circle of friends, recalled in an interview that when he moved to Los Angeles he "thought the movies were quite frivolous." He recalled, "The older generation of my time had no feeling of respect for the movies" (155). Nonetheless, like Boxley or James M. Cain, he quickly learned that the commonplace notions regarding the writer in Hollywood were untrue. "I object, for instance," he said, "to the notion that F. Schott Fitzgerald was ruined by Hollywood" (166). Instead of writing the worst work he could dream up for movie-going folks and simpletons, he stated, "I always wrote for the most intelligent people I could think of" and he added, "I always believed you had to do your very best, that you never should write down to an audience [...]" (163).

Fine includes Fante in his list of "Eastern Writers in Hollywood, 1927-1940" (161-162). This is Fine's only mention of Fante. Fante, born in Colorado, did not journey east until well beyond his formative years. Although as a young man he moved westward, his aesthetic sense remained shaped by an East Coast notion of the author. In his essay on California poet Robinson Jeffers, Dana Gioia has written: "Has any American author ever been able to build and sustain a major literary presence from the West Coast? As writers from Allen Ginsburg to Joan Didion know, if one lives out West, one must also keep an apartment in Manhattan" (57). Fante had no New York address. His mentor H. L. Mencken, however, was his East Coast connection. In 1934 he advised Fante to secure a literary agent in New York even though "agents in most cases are unnecessary" (*Fante / Mencken* 77). Fante needed an agent in New York because of the great distance that separates it from Los Angeles. That this could be a distance in understanding as well as in miles did not occur to the self-assured Mencken and so in this same letter he also advised Fante, "I see no reason whatever why you shouldn't get something from the movie magnates in order to finance the work you want to do" (77).

Frank Spotnitz concludes in an essay published six years after Fante's death, "The Hottest Dead Man in Hollywood," "Perhaps a sense that the movies Fante depended on financially were responsible for aborting his literary ambitions helps explain his abiding distaste for Hollywood" (54). He speculates that "the studios [...] thwarted what could have been one of the great literary careers of this century" (54). Fante certainly condemns Hollywood from the time of his earliest letters to his last. A better explanation for Fante's "abiding distaste," however, may be Fine's explanation for some writers' frequently stated dislike of the industry. "Writers' reactions to the studio system," he says "[...] only make sense in light of the beliefs, attitudes, and values attendant to the identity 'writer' that these individuals had learned in New York's literary marketplace, for it is the consistency with which writers judged Hollywood in terms of New York that seems the operant factor in their experiences in the studios" (104). A better explanation for Fante's "thwarted" literary career than the studios' exploitation of him, might be the author's own misconceptions of screenwriting, rigid belief in the supremacy of the novel, and destructive behavior: drinking, gambling, and spending.

In his early fiction (*The Road to Los Angeles*; *Wait Until Spring, Bandini*; and *Ask the Dust*) and in later fiction about his early life (*1933 Was a Bad Year*), Fante makes little mention of the movies. It makes sense not to describe screenwriting in these fictions since they trace the early life of alter ego Arturo Bandini / Dominic Molise from adolescence in Colorado to early adulthood in Los Angeles. Yet, what he does say about the movies in these stories is significant for in these fictions films are one of several illusions that distort life in America. In the later work, *1933 Was a Bad Year*, sports and movies are mixed-up with religion in "a house full of dreamers" (36). Dominic finds an envelope stuffed full with pictures of movie actress Carole Lombard under his brother August's pillow. He quickly understands why August maintained such secrecy about these photographs: "Some of the portraits were signed in his own handwriting 'For my darling August, adoringly—Carole'" (35). He realizes that his brother dreams of Carole Lombard "as fiercely as I dreamed of baseball" (36). When Dominic has a vision of the Virgin Mary he believes that "for a moment [...] it was Carole Lombard" (37). Sports, movies, and religion offer the Molises a possible way out of their life of poverty, but their roadmap, for Fante, is a forgery like August's false signature of Lombard's name.

In *The Road to Los Angeles* neither movies and sports nor religion are the vehicle used for the displacement of responsibility. Instead, Nietzschean philosophy becomes the orthodoxy that curtails self-fulfillment for the immature and struggling young author, Arturo Bandini. While a cannery worker and stinking of fish, Arturo goes one night to the movies. "I sat by myself," he says, "all alone in the corner, my smell and I." Soon, he says, "People all around me got up and moved away." Arturo does not go to the movies after this. He says that he "didn't mind" because the others in the audience "were rabble anyhow." So he stays home and reads "books the rabble can't read [...] most of them very hard to understand, some of them so dull I had to pretend they were fascinating [...]" (84-85)—so much for the young author, the young Arturo as Superman. Zarathustra said, "'I teach you the overman [Superman]. Man is something that shall be overcome. What have you done to overcome him'" (Nietzsche 124). Arturo avoided the moviehouse, stayed home, and read dull books.

In *Wait Until Spring, Bandini* he refers to movies as "that celluloid drug," and in his "Prologue to Ask the Dust" he emphasizes that his Los Angeles fiction will not be the story of Hollywood glamour.

> Do I speak of Hollywood with its tinsel blah? of the movies? Do I speak of Bel Air and Lakeside? Do I speak of Pasadena and the hot spots herea-

bouts?—no and no a thousand times. I tell you this is a book about a girl and a boy in a different civilization: this is about Main Street and Spring Street and Bunker Hill, about the town no farther west than Figueroa.... (147)

In his fiction of the thirties he moved "no farther west than Figueroa," in his letters of this period, especially those addressed to his mother or his father figure H. L. Mencken, he seldom moved east of it. These letters make it very clear that Fante had imbued what Fine describes as the East Coast writers' attitudes and beliefs regarding the profession of authorship. Furthermore, his friendship with Hollywood authors such as Ross Wills encouraged Fante to maintain these beliefs and hence these friendships fostered a pre-existent prejudice against the film industry.

In 1935 Fante told his mother: "In many ways I wish I had never worked for the movies. They have a tendency to spoil a good writer. [...] I am anxious to forget the pictures now, forget the easy living and big salaries of picture people, and live only for my book" (*Selected Letters* 108). Yet, in the very next sentence he added, "When that is published my value to pictures will increase a hundredfold" (108). The "big money" that he hasn't yet seen will be guaranteed when his book appears. Conversely, in a journal he kept during 1940 he recorded that his publisher "does not know, the sucker, that I have a sold a movie original. [...] I have to laugh when I think of the rude shock he gets when he learns my terms for a new book" ("John Fante's Diary" 320). Fante believed that publishing his novel would give added value to any movie-writing contract, but also that movie-writing could be used as leverage for a book contract.

During this period Fante told Mencken "what I want most from art is money" (*Fante / Mencken* 110). The balance that any commercial aesthetic requires proved difficult for Fante to negotiate. Film work, he told Mencken, is "a nerve-racking, jittery existence and in the last analysis not worthwhile. The compromise becomes increasingly difficult. Hollywood is a bad place. It kills writers. They die young and violently down here" (*Fante / Mencken* 103).

Fante scholars all too readily mimic the voice of their subject even when attempting to reveal a changing attitude about or relationship between the author and Hollywood. In his section introduction for Fante's 1940s letters, for example, *Selected Letters* editor Seamus Cooney twice uses the word "temptations" in one sentence about the film industry. For Fante scholars the film industry is never a place of employment (neutral) or a place of opportunity (positive), but always either a threat (negative) or the devil incarnate.

Stephen Cooper says at one point that Fante learned "that the constraints of the [film] business, if not completely inflexible, could be suffocating enough" (118). A mere four pages before this Cooper observes that Knopf rejected a Fante manuscript, "refusing so much as to recognize the manuscript of *In My Time* [*The Road to Los Angeles*] as a novel" (114). While Cooper paints the constraints of film writing as "suffocating," he does not do so for the book industry.

Fante told Mencken that "the book was truly a bad novel, and no one would have got any good out of its publication" (*Fante / Mencken* 75). In a later letter he told his mentor, "If Knopf has a bad taste in his mouth as far as I'm concerned, I certainly have no one to blame but myself" (*Fante / Mencken* 97). Bad novel writing, then, results from the inadequacies of a particular author whereas the shoddiness of scripts results from the idiocies of bumbling producers. That, too, is part of the writer-in-Hollywood legend. As Fine explains, "The 'real' writer possessed autonomy, hence it is not surprising the Eastern writers felt it impossible to be a 'real' writer in Hollywood, where ownership rights were signed away on the dotted line and creative control lay in the producer's hands" (122). According to Fine's analysis of the legend, "instead of receiving prestige because they were writers, they found themselves denied prestige because of their profession" (128). So a number of writers-in-Hollywood believed. As Cecelia Brady (a producer's daughter) puts it in Fitzgerald's *The Last Tycoon*, "I grew up thinking that writer and secretary were the same, except that a writer usually smelled of cocktails and came more often to meals" (99).

As late as the sixties and seventies Fante would be hard on the film-industry and easy on the publishing industry. In 1965 he told Carey McWilliams, "I am still writing movies. I have escaped TV, but all my friends have been flushed down, including Fenton, who actually sits down dead drunk at his machine and grinds the stuff out" (*Selected Letters* 288). And in 1971 he wrote McWilliams, "The rejection by Grove Press [of *My Dog Stupid*] is dismal news of course, but I am not discouraged. Somewhere in that publishing jungle my little book will surely find a home" (289).

In the following decade, the 1980s, when Fante looked back at his early years in Los Angeles in his final novel, *Dreams from Bunker Hill*, he described his alter ego's, Arturo Bandini, beginnings as a screenwriter in the Hollywood film industry. Arturo gets his introduction through a fellow screenwriter named Frank Edgington, a composite character based on Frank Fenton, Joel Sayre, and other Hollywood writers that Fante knew. If Fante showed intimations of taking films seriously when he first arrived and if it might have been possible for him to become a screenwriter like Philip Dunne, his acquaintances quickly slammed that possibility shut and bolstered the Hollywood as destroyer image. In January 1933 Fante told his mother: "My scenario with M.G.M. is still out there, and I haven't heard a word about it. It was probably rejected. [...] Well, I'm not discouraged. I have plenty of time, and I'm learning every day" (*Fante Reader* 289). Just a short time later, though, he told Mencken that Sayre "knows more about movies than any man in this town and he can write them standing on his head. I have learned a lot from him" (90). These were the wrong lessons to learn. "Sayre," Cooper says, "who would rather play poker than write, urged him [Fante] to take it easy" (122). And when young Arturo walks into Edgington's office he asks, "'What are you working on?'" "'A piece of crap,'" Edgington replies. Edgington, Arturo tells us, was an Eastern writer who "hated Hollywood" (46). Instead of writing, Arturo recalls, "we drank beer and played the pinball games" (47).

Later in the story, when Arturo teams up with Velda van der Zee, he works prodigiously on a script. Edgington's agent, Cyril Korn, tells Arturo that co-authoring a script with Velda will be a great opportunity and he will certainly receive a screen credit. Arturo accepts. He does all the work on the script. "I was on to something touched with greatness" (88). He sends it off to Velda with much pride and enthusiasm. Fifteen weeks later he hears from his colleague. She reassures Arturo that she has made very few changes in his well-wrought script. When he next sees the script he says, "I was down the first page halfway when my hair began to stiffen. In the middle of the second page I was forced to put the script aside and hang on to the porch banister" (89). Arturo has been betrayed, betrayed not by a bumbling producer but by another Hollywood writer.

In order to maintain his integrity he has his name removed from the script, a script which does get produced and hence Arturo does not receive the guaranteed and coveted screen credit that he so desperately needs. Fante's brilliant satire does not end here. When Arturo first meets Velda she overwhelms him with a non-stop and nonsensical monologue about Hollywood celebrities. In the penultimate chapter of the book while attending a party back home in Colorado, Arturo, drunk, uses a long list of others to rescue his own name. "I play golf with Bing Crosby [...]. I swim with Johnny Weismuller [...]. Everybody loves me" (142). It doesn't work. He impresses no one. He loses all integrity.

It is not only near the end of the novel that Arturo's behavior undermines his desires. From the very start of it, it is Arturo's inept behavior that ruins his every chance to be a writer. Near the novel's start he secures employment with a literary agent. He rewrites a client's story. Then he receives criticism and blame when the unhappy client complains. He gets a second chance to work with the client, lies to her and tells her he went to church to beg forgiveness for the hatchet job he did on her story; then he makes a pass at her, and this time the boss fires him.

Fante's most self-critical examination of his alter ego as screenwriter (remember in his "Prologue to *Ask the Dust*" he said "[...] I, John Fante and Arturo Bandini, two in one [...]" [144]) occurs in the novella *My Dog Stupid* (completed in 1971). The house in this story resembles Fante's own Point Dume residence and in this fiction he says, "the entire layout looked exactly like what it was not—the domicile of a successful writer" (11). Henry J. Molise refers to his film work as "miserable screenplays" (17). Among his reasons for keeping the stray dog Stupid are the following: "I was tired of defeat and failure. I hungered for victory. [...] Stupid was victory, the books I had not written [...]" (42). His screenplays he twice refers to as "cop-outs" (100, 109). In other words, the fault was his and not the studios'. His son, Denny, tells him, "'Dad, you're a lousy writer,'" and then adds, "'I've read your novels. They're corny, sentimental cop-outs, and I'm not even talking about your screenplays'" (70). As the conversation proceeds, Henry gradually tries to defend his literary reputation.

> "The screenplays aren't much," I admitted.
> "Why did you ever become a writer, Dad? How the hell did you ever get published?"
> "Oh, shit. I'm not that bad! H. L. Mencken thought I was pretty good. He published me first."
> "You stink, Dad, you really do."
> "*The Tyrant* isn't a bad book. It got great reviews."
> "How many copies did it sell?'
> "Not many, but it made a pretty good movie." (70)

It's a waste of life and talent to write for Hollywood, Henry believes, but, paradoxically, it is a compliment to have one's novel turned into film.

At one point near the middle of the story Henry explains some perceived differences between screenwriting and novel writing. A month after the arrival of Stupid, Henry begins a novel. "Nothing unusual about that," he says. "I began novels all the time, filling the gaps between screen assignments. But they petered out for lack of confidence and discipline, and I abandoned them with a sense of relief" (55). Thirty years before

Ross Wills had observed in his profile of Fante, "As a worker at the job of writing, he is rather lazy and easily distracted" (337). Henry follows the above quoted passage with his discussion of screenwriting and novel writing. He says the former is easy, lucrative, formulaic, and "When finished you gave it to other people who tore it to pieces trying to put it on film" (55). Novel writing, on the other hand, he says, is an "awesome" responsibility and if your novel fails, you have only yourself to blame. This rigid and long-lasting expressed belief in the legends of the film and book industries seems especially strange here since when *Ask the Dust* appeared its promotion never took place because at that time Adolf Hitler had sued Fante's publisher, Stackpole Sons. How could the author blame only himself for the limited success of his work in such a circumstance? How could he not see that both film-writing and novel writing required discipline and that market-place forces affected both the writing of scripts and the writing of novels?

In several early letters regarding the sale of short stories Fante mentioned having been "gypped" (*Selected Letters* 43), having not received any payment (*Selected Letters* 66), having had a lucky break when a rejected story received reconsideration and acceptance after Fante made use of the influence of others, and referred to peddling his fiction and the uncertainty of it all (*Selected Letters* 68). In other words, beliefs regarding filmmaking and publishing were so ingrained, so firm that no amount of lived-experience could shake them. A story he planned to submit to Warner Brothers would have a very uncertain chance of making it to the screen, Fante told his mother in 1934 (*Selected Letters* 89). In his 1940 diary he wrote:

> Had a letter from Soskin [his editor at Stockpole] yesterday. He wants another novel from me, of course. His letter very unsatisfactory. He has started a new firm and is characteristically excited. But he has fooled me too often in the past. (321)

Fante never saw any similarities between the businesses of films and books: that both had uncertainties, for example, or that both had aspects of economic necessities and artistic ideals. Even if Fante believed Soskin, he may not have been able to send him anything. In 1935 he told his mother that "I much prefer getting through the novel" than working for the movies (*Selected Letters* 96). Yet, at the time he wrote his mother he hadn't worked on his novel all year and used his sporadic film employment as his reason or excuse.

Soon he had other reasons for avoiding work on his fiction. As he told Ben Pleasants in his final interview, "Well, I pissed away a few years of my life [...]" (95). He mentioned "golf, reading, dallying with one novel and then another" (95), but to this list could be added impulsive spending, excessive drinking, and high-stakes gambling. In *My Dog Stupid* after rereading a work-in-progress and realizing that "it wasn't a novel at all," but "a detailed screen treatment, a flat, sterile one-dimensional blueprint of a movie" (74), Henry makes a list of his vices: "regularly observed at the liquor store [...] Of walking the beach [...] Wanders aimlessly in his yard, chipping golf balls with a nine iron" (75). Ironically, he begins this critical self-examination with a line adapted from *Citizen Kane*: "So, as it must to all men, death came to Henry J. Molise" (75). (The final line of the newsreel sequence in the film is: "Then, last week, as it must to all men, death came to Charles Foster Kane.")

In *Full of Life* the character "John Fante," at home with his pregnant wife, checks with his film studio secretary: "My calls were routine. Somebody wanted to play golf, and somebody else wanted to play poker" (87))—thus, was his routine. And in *The Brotherhood of the Grape* while up north at Sam Ramponi's motel about to begin assisting his father build a smokehouse, Henry Molise thinks about home in Los Angeles and that if he were there he'd be starting, instead of hard masonry work with his father, "altogether a dreamy day of rest and calculated indolence, putting off an hour or two of work to the late afternoon when it could no longer be avoided" (110). Such is not the disciplined schedule of either a dedicated screenwriter or novelist.

In his letters Fante made some infrequent references to his distracting habits whereas he so frequently complained, as John Gregory Dunne presumptuously put it, about the "Monster," Hollywood. In 1946 Fante told his mother that his work on a new book proceeded very slowly. He said, "At this rate, it'll take a year to write the damned thing. And yet, I don't care much. I play golf every day, and so long as I am able to do that I don't worry about anything else" (*Selected Letters* 214). The following year he told his mother and father, "I have been having considerable trouble writing lately. I have gone stale, and it's hard work. But it's really my fault. For two years now I have played golf every day, and my work has suffered" (*Selected Letters* 218). Such confessions, however, are exceptions to the usual complaints. Furthermore, in these confessions he says nothing of profligate spending, drunken folly, or habitual gambling.

In his *American Mercury* minority opinion James M. Cain said that Hollywood did not bear the guilt for destroying writers. Rather, Cain believed, some authors condemned themselves to failure and then turned around and blamed "their troubles on" the studios that employed them (140). Fante could not consciously and fully understand the similarities between two businesses: film production and book production. He couldn't, for to do so would have ruined the unhappy screenwriter's "most frequent out" (Cain 140). In addition, Fante judged his West Coast situation with East Coast ideals. Cooper mars his otherwise excellent biography of Fante with the perpetuation of the writer-in-Hollywood legend. At one point he addresses Fante's bad habits and during his discussion of them he writes, "No matter how therapeutic the hours spent walking the fairways, addressing the ball and watching its flight, the sheer amount of time he poured into the game over the next several years took its toll in other areas of his life" (218). But like Fante himself Cooper often writes of "the temptation to backslide into the Hollywood morass of 'original story' writing" (160), as if screenwriting, too, were an addiction and not a possibility, never mind an art.

Ross Wills speculated about his friend John Fante: "Probably his worst time-consumer is pin-ball." Wills continued, "I don't know how many dollars and hours he has flung away trying to 'raise the American flag' on these machines. But his joy when he does so is triumphant—greater than that experienced at the publication of a new book. When he just misses, his gloom and despair are crushing" (337). Maybe Fante has beaten the literary marbles game at last. Despair no more. His literary rescuer, John Martin of Black Sparrow Press, sold the rights to Fante's books to the Ecco Press, an imprint of Harper-Collins. They'll have a budget sufficient to manufacture an audience for these products, a budget big enough to raise high the Fante flag.

Chapter 7

PAGANO'S GOLD

Jo Pagano (1906-1982) was one of the early West Coast Italian American writers. In his literary work he sang a one-note song in two different registers. From an early short story such as "The Disinherited" (1934) to his 1947 crime-story *The Condemned* he frequently wrote about the same autobiographically inspired characters, especially the Simone family, similar to the way John Fante wrote of the Bandini (or Molise) family. Indeed, Jerre Mangione compared the short story collections by these two ex-Colorado Southern Californian writing friends in a 1941 *New Republic* review. Yet, unlike Fante, Pagano struck literary gold only once. *Golden Wedding*, his 1943 novel, is his best work and far better than his 1940 short story collection, *The Paesanos*, *The Condemned*, or the episodes he later wrote for TV shows such as *Bonanza*. Pagano's Italian American novel tells the story of fifty years in the life of married couple Luigi and Marietta Simone. As Pagano put it: "The history of their life was the history of an era, a dozen eras" (248). The genius of this novel is its style combined with an uplifting narrative of ethnic particularity and national generality. Furthermore, whereas *The Paesanos* perpetuates ethnic stereotypes and the author's ethnic themes become secondary in the generic conventions of *The Condemned*, *Golden Wedding*, like Jerre Mangione's family memoir-novel of approximately the same moment (1942), counters ethnic stereotypes.

From his first fictional writings Pagano usually focused on the autobiographically based Simone family. The stories are most often first person narratives told from the perspective of Robert Simone: a former student of medicine, a young practicing physician, or an older physician. This alter-ego narrator ages as the author himself ages. In the 1934 story "The Disinherited" Robert had to forsake his aspirations due to the economic crisis of the Depression (321). In 1947's *The Condemned* Dr. Simone is a visitor to the main character's house. Gil is a newspaper writer and would be author of "serious" books. The third-person narrator of this murder mystery notes that Dr. Simone "had written, some three or four years before, a novel about his family which had received very little attention [...]" (104). It was "a melancholy novelette called *Death of a Brother*" (104). This is the title of the final short story in Pagano's *The Paesanos*. Both the actual story and the intertextually referenced novelette are about "the brilliant young painter, Carl Simone, who had been killed in Spain fighting against the Fascists [...]" (*Condemned* 104).

Carl Simone, too, might be an alter ego for the author. The obituary published in *Variety* in April 1982 notes that as well as writing, Pagano began his career as a commercial illustrator. The main character of *The Condemned* might also be based in Pagano's own life experience even though this novel has an atypical third person narration that might thus seem to offer distance between author and character. For Gil's newspaper work could be seen as a metaphor for Pagano's Hollywood film and television writing, an employment that kept the author away from his "art." Gil's wife says to her husband: "'When I think of the things you could *really* write if you had the time!'" She asks, "'Gil, *why* don't you quit?'" Gil, who is the star investigative reporter for his newspaper, replies that his editor is always "'giving me a bonus—.'" Money—that old curse of the writer in Hollywood. His wife replies, "'To hell with the bonus. [...] Darling, the book's the important thing'" (60). In the prior chapter I showed how Fante's career and writings illustrate and complicate standard notions of the writer in Hollywood and how one Italian American author navigated the blurred intersections of art and commerce. In *The Condemned* there is none of the intense bitterness (regarding journalism) that one finds in Fante's letters to friends and family regarding Hollywood employment and its supposed destructiveness for literary writing.

Pagano and Fante became friends very early in their Hollywood careers. Both authors had Italian American and Colorado roots and both authors strove to gain entry into the worlds of literary publication and profitable film work. Pagano introduced Fante to colleagues in the entertainment industry. As Fante expressed in a letter of 25 November 1932 addressed to his mother: "Last week Joe took me out to different people in Hollywood, and I met many interesting and likable folks, and had a wonderful time through it all. Joe is a writer too, and he knows many others like ourselves" (*Selected Letters* 33). Furthermore, in this letter he informed his mother that he "spent Thanksgiving with the Paganos. A huge dinner: Spaghetti, turkey, la basola (that's bad spelling), Denver celery, and all the good things which I like so well" (*Selected Letters* 33).

Yet, by 1 January 1934 he told his mother of his reservations regarding his friend's writing ability. "I was the only person honest enough to tell Pagano his book was not worth a whoop" (*Selected Letters* 70). Perhaps, Pagano years later served as the model for the character Joe Crispi in *My Dog Stupid*. Like Pagano's father, the fictional Crispi's father had worked in mining. Like Pagano the fictional Crispi had once published a novel about Italian Americans. Crispi is now a television producer who has a new show in the works "titled, 'Lucky Pierre'"[...]. Fante writes, "the hero was a dog, a fucking little French poodle named Pierre" (*Stupid* 49). Fante's autobiographically based narrator and protagonist Henry Molise, nonetheless, briefly considers writing for his old friend and fellow writer now turned producer even though Crispi's show makes Molise feel like he'll "vomit or die" (50).

When their short story collections appeared in the same year the young Italian American writer Jerre Mangione reviewed them together for the *New Republic*. He found much to praise in both collections but he concluded: "Although Pagano seems to have richer material, his stories lack the variety of mood and treatment of those in 'Dago Red' [by Fante]."

Many years after its initial publication, Mangione reconsidered his motives for writing *Mount Allegro: A Memoir of Italian American Life* (1942). In his "Finale" written for the 1981 edition of *Mount Allegro* he recalled "the hope that I could produce a work that might help dispel some of the more spurious clichés pinned to the image of Italian Americans by an uninformed American public" (302). Dispelling erroneous beliefs about Italian Americans became especially important and urgent in the early 1940s when America went to war against Italy. At the conclusion of both *Mount Allegro* and *Golden Wedding* a reader today can clearly see patriotic appeals. Also, *Golden Wedding*, like *Mount Allegro*, succeeds at painting a just picture of Italian Americans. *The Paesanos*, however, does not. Rather than counter stereotypes, this short story collection perpetuates gross inaccuracies and belittles the ethnic group of which Pagano was a part.

The reviewer of *The Paesanos* for *The New York Times* called the work "one of those delightful groupings of genre pieces where sentiment lies unobtrusive and genuine beneath rollicking laughter and reality is not denied by the wildest extravagance" (Woods). But I believe that reality had been sacrificed for the sake of laughter. In Pagano's attempt at humor, reality became lost and Italian Americans, more lampooned than depicted.

The ethnic characters of these fictions are for the most part no different than the immigrants stereotypically and derisively described by Jacob Riis in 1890: "He is as honest as he is hot-headed. [...] The Italian is gay, lighthearted and, if his fur is not stroked the wrong way, inoffensive as a child" (45). These words well describe George Beban's Beppo (1915) and also they well describe Pagano's character Gianpaolo Maccalucci, best friend of Luigi Simone. In almost every story Gianpaolo is quick to anger and effortlessly drags Luigi into his battles. His is not a violent hot-temper, but rather one of child-like qualities and buffoonery. In one story, for example, Gianpaolo, knife in hand, chases a bothersome cousin out of his house. In "Roman Holiday" Gianpaolo loses his temper and then gets so excited he cannot speak. Next he punches someone "in the nose" (186). Then "Malpighi struck back—and at that moment a half-dozen waiters plunged into the fray. They all pounced on Gianpaolo at once." Gianpaolo shouts, "'Helpa! Helpa!'" Immigrant males in this story collection always speak in an absurd Italian-English dialect. It is more cartoon-like, than realist. The narrator —Robert—next says: "and then my father lumbered into action...." (186). More waiters enter the fray and then "with one movement the men in our party plunged into the milling mob" (187).

Not all of the stories are as silly, though. The title story and "Ceasar at the Feast" have their appealing qualities and "Awinding We Did Go" has a very particular Californian aspect to it. In this road trip story the combined Maccalucci and Simone families do not reach the destination of their outing: "Paradise Valley" and so here, even though it has its share of slapstick silliness, there is a profundity as well.

The final story of the ten is especially interesting for its relation to *Golden Wedding* and *The Condemned* and for its approach to war in Europe from an American European immigrant perspective. This story is the "novelette" briefly mentioned in *The Condemned*. Pagano exaggerates a bit, for it is only twenty pages. Between the story collection and *Golden Wedding* he reworked the "melancholy" events of the main character and narrator's younger brother's death. I believe he did so to offer clearer support—Italian American support—for the Allied war effort. Robert Simone's younger brother Carl and Carl's teacher, John Feld, appear in all three works, but interestingly the stereotypically described buffoon Gianpaolo Maccalucci, while central to *The Paesanos*, appears only very briefly in the celebratory scene that concludes *Golden Wedding* and is mentioned one other time in the novel. (He disappears completely from the pages of *The Condemned*.) Global conflagration left little room, perhaps, for Maccaluccian ethnic humor.

Whereas at the conclusion of "Death of a Brother" Carl enlists in the anti-Fascist International Brigade in large part due to revenge motives (his pregnant wife, Stella, had been killed in a Fascist bombardment), in the later work he fights only for idealistic reasons. Granted, in the story Carl states in a letter to his brother:

> if I die, remember that I died as I would wish to die—for reason, for light, for all those ideals which we in America were bred on, and which we cannot allow to perish from the face of the earth. (229)

The call to arms quickly gets completely undercut by Feld's letter that describes Carl's death:

> "[...] a detachment of Italians were upon us. Carl and another Italian met hand to hand with bayonets. [...] Carl was run through. I bludgeoned the other Italian, and he fell on top of Carl. [...] he was only a boy, no more than eighteen. He looked at me pleadingly: I could not go through with it. I carried them both to a barn, and they died there together." (230)

This melodramatic depiction of the horrors of war undercuts the last words from Carl. Furthermore, whereas *The Paesanos* ends with the deaths of Stella and Carl and also mother Marietta Simone's funeral, *Golden Wedding* concludes with an anniversary celebration. Life will go on the latter work intimates and that is one of the reasons to curtail stereotypes and to support the war effort.

Near the end of his 1942 memoir *Mount Allegro* Jerre Mangione recalls asking himself a series of questions after he read a number of books that advocated for the melting pot theory of immigration and assimilation. "Was it in the chemistry of human life for my relatives to become Anglo-Saxonized," he asks, for example (239)? He concludes with a plea for cultural pluralism: "Didn't America need their wisdom and their warmth, just as they and their children needed America's youth and vigor?" (239). We can learn and prosper together, according to Mangione, and without absorbing difference into an indistinguishable sameness.

However, in the 1930s there grew an ever-increasing threat to any possible pluralism: Fascism. In the summer of 1936 young Jerre Mangione breaks the bounds of neighborhood and family and travels to Italy.

"I would know with my own eyes," he says, "what the flesh of Fascism was like" (240). He doesn't like what he sees. "I shuddered [...]," he recalls, "for the patriots who would some day have to face the truth about their black-shirted heroes" (255). In other words, after offering an implicit defense of all Italian Americans, he then criticizes many Italians. He even uses a bit of humor in doing the latter, noting that he left one town "on a train that was a half-hour late" (264), and thus pokes fun at the Fascist claim regarding punctuality of rail service. The title of the last chapter: "Blighted Land." Mangione makes Italian Americans look good and notes the many failings of the Italian Fascists. In 1942, therefore, this personal account had a very public function.

Similarly, Pagano produced his 1943 novel with some mildly propagandistic purposes in mind. He, too, narrates an unbiased account of an Italian American family and he, too, concludes his volume in a manner that had some resonance for its contemporary audience. As previously noted, the story of younger brother Carl differs here from its earlier telling and so, too, does the context in which Robert situates it. Once again Carl, his wife Stella and teacher, mentor, and fellow artist John Feld travel to Spain when war breaks out. This time both Carl and Stella speak lines that could have easily been part of the film-script for *Casablanca*; that is, if we take the war in Spain as analogous to the more widespread war in Europe that followed. Carl tells Robert in a letter:

> "Bob, all of you who live in the peace and comparative security of a still free America, you simply can't imagine what is happening here. You can't imagine the sublime heroism of these determined people, struggling against all imaginable odds to free themselves from tyranny. The part that Mussolini and his Fascist barbarians are playing in the monstrous rape of these people has made me for the first time almost ashamed that I am an Italian. But there are many Italians here fighting the Fascists. There are Italians from Italy, there are Italians from America. It is a common struggle, and it is heroic in scope. Hitler, whom we so long underestimated in America, is trying out his war machine here, and it is horrible to contemplate. He must be defeated, and Mussolini with him." (281-282)

The message is clear. At first Carl goes to Spain to bear witness as an artist. He returns home for his parents' golden wedding anniversary celebration. But he has made up his mind to return to Spain and fight this time with sword instead of brush—unless Stella asks him not to fight. Stella confides in older brother Robert during the celebration:

> "Those beasts, those unutterable Nazi and Fascist beasts....! No, I promised myself I wouldn't talk about it. If you had seen the way they slaughtered innocent civilians! Simple, good people, people like your mother and father... That's what they're trying to stamp out, everything that people like your mother and father mean in this world—the simple, good things, the decent, human things. ..." (298)

Robert replies that he understands and that she seems to be seeking "'reassurance'" (298). Stella notes, "'I can stop him [Carl] from going. He will not go if I tell him not to. He told me he would not. What shall I tell him?'" (299). Robert turns the question back to Stella and she says that she wants to tell her husband "'to fight'" (299). Robert emphasizes: "'Then that is what you must tell him'" (299).

How different this scene is from the one that concludes "Death of a Brother." Here there is no motivation based on melodramatic revenge. Here there is no ambivalence resulting from war's waste and horror. Here instead of a funeral as the context for a recounting of distant events we have a celebration of a fifty-year marriage and a renewal of wedding vows. The book concludes with the wedding march and not a military one and yet both marches are indicative of commitment.

Pagano's depiction of California in *Golden Wedding* is also optimistic, patriotic, and bright. It, too, provides a reason to celebrate life and to fight for the way of life that is celebrated. Although the Simones and Maccaluccis do not reach "Paradise Valley" in "Awinding We Did Go," the Simones do reach a West Coast wonderland in the later work. Virtually halfway through the narrative Marietta visits her daughter Rose in California to help with the birth of a grandchild. Robert, at this point a young boy, accompanies his mother on the long train trip. "'I wish we'd hurry up and get to California,'" he whines at one point (144). They begin to see palm trees and orange groves. The conductor comes by and Marietta asks when they'll reach California. "'California!'" he said. 'Lady, we been in California for hours'" (144). "California!" Robert narrates retrospectively if not nostalgically, "It was as though we had stumbled without knowing it into paradise" (144).

The entire third section of the three-part novel (207-300) takes place in California. Earlier sections occur in Colorado and Utah. This telling of the Simone story has them weathering the Depression and Robert does complete his medical education. This is the opposite of "The Disinherited." In 1943 one had to go to war for prosperity and paradise, not for despair and decay. Pagano's California has idealistic qualities to it. This is so much different from Italian author Cesare Pavese's imagined California. Pavese's post-war novel *The Moon and The Bonfires* paints a harshly realistic picture of the state. The nameless narrator, as Italian immigrant, asks, "Was it worth it to have come? Where could I go now? Throw myself off the breakwater?" (16). In California, he says, "There were women, there was land, there was money. But nobody had enough, nobody stopped no matter how much he had [...] fake flower beds [...] or else wilderness, burned over land, mountains of slag" (16). And so he returns to Italy. Pagano and the Simones of *Golden Wedding* see a different California, a truly "Golden Land," not in the ironic sense that William Faulkner used that phrase for a short-story title. And the people of California are as Stella describes Robert's parents: simple, good, decent, and human. The Simones are part of this population. They are not ridiculed through stereotype and made to stand separate from the rest of their community or nation, despite the many customs unique to their ethnic group.

Pagano uses a chronological order of events, though he elides some years and analyzes others. The three part novel of eighteen chapters depicts scenes in detail and relates family stories. Occasionally, Pagano incorporates poetic phrasing, but more often it is the simple and direct plain style that propels the narrative.

Part One, five chapters running from page three to seventy-one, relates the meeting of Luigi and Marietta, their marriage and early life together in the mining town of Coalville, Colorado and then in nearby Rockton. Within a year they move again; this time to Denver. Luigi has moved from the mines to co-ownership of a saloon to produce merchandizing. For Marietta, "Always in the back of her mind, was this driving urge to gain greater advantages for the children" (41). Curiously, whereas Marietta never speaks with an accent, Luigi at first does and then does so only on rare occasions when he becomes angry and finally and thankfully by the end of this section, his accent disappears. "'It'sa pretty dark and the sky, she'sa filled with stars," exemplifies his idiolect spoken earlier in the novel and throughout most of *The Paesanos*.

Whereas Marietta thinks of securing advantages for the children, Luigi contemplates material plenitude.

> He loved to prowl about in stores, fingering the gleaming knives and silverware, admiring the bolts of wool and silk and cotton prints, memorizing laboriously the American name for each object; and he loved to feast his eyes on the great barrels of crackers and dried fish and flour, the slippery slabs of bacon and salt-pork, the cans of olives and peppers and tomatoes and oil, all of which filled him with a contented sense of plentitude. (12-13)

Whether educational advantages for one's children or prosperity for oneself and one's family are sought, these are very common national urges and desires.

More unique to the Italian experience is one of the threats to the Simone family's aspirations. While in Denver, the Black Hand threatens them. At Marietta's urging, they move once again. This time they move to Salt Lake City, Utah where Luigi once more becomes a saloonkeeper.

In Part Two—seven chapters running from page seventy-five to two-hundred and three—the major scenes include Rose's wedding, the first Simone child to form a family of her own. While an event such as this provides another common and shared aspect of life in the narrative, the story of Robert's brother Lou has uniqueness to it in that he is a boxer and a prodigal son. Robert and a friend go to see Lou fight. "It was not fun at all," Robert recalls, "—to the contrary, it was the most miserable night, I thought, that I had ever spent. The many voices had become concentrated into one voice, a horrible, screaming, bloodthirsty voice: and the many faces were one face—the face of the fat man next to me, flushed, brutal, with bulging eyes and a blubbering mouth" (121). At the end of this section of the novel, Lou dies, a soldier fighting for America in the First World War.

Lou's death is anticipated by another death, and the pain of war is brought home by the incident that causes it. Robert takes violin lessons from Professor Alessandro Berardi. The Professor has an argument and fight with his German neighbor, Ernest Johansen. The disagreement ends tragically with the Professor's death. Robert recalls: "The actual world was the world which I had seen, felt, tasted from the day of my birth, and which, each day, I was growing into with an ever greater awareness. The other worlds were vague, glamorous and dreamlike. [...] That the war could reach over from the other dreamlike world into the world of my own awareness shocked and confused me" (175-176).

When Prohibition becomes the law of the land the Simones once again make a move. From the saloon business Luigi returns to produce —this time in Los Angeles, California. Part Three—six chapters running from page two-hundred and seven to three-hundred—describes events from the time of their move through the Depression and to Luigi's retirement and the second wedding of Luigi and Marietta on their Golden Wedding anniversary. Unlike the early short story written during economic turmoil, "The Disinherited," here the Simones weather the Depression. "Dark months, bitter months; months of bewilderment and confusion," (249) Robert states, but they do survive and in this novel, unlike the earlier story, Robert does attain his M.D. degree. The family loses some investments and the family retains other investments.

As noted earlier, this optimistic approach works well to establish a context for Carl's story. One Simone son has died fighting for his country and another will set off to fight new battles in a new global conflict. Unlike "Death of a Brother," *Golden Wedding* does not conclude with a patriot's death.

Also adding to the establishment of the positive context is Pagano's depiction of California. Golden land opportunity enables reunification of the family. Rose and her husband and children take advantage of a business opportunity and move from Fresno to the same Los Angeles neighborhood as the Simones. Robert opens up a small hospital with two former classmates. California in *Golden Wedding* is all golden opportunity.

Yes, opportunities abound in Southern California. It was this sense of possibility that drew the Simones from Salt Lake City to Los Angeles. Robert recalls what he found upon arrival:

> Our house stood on rising ground at the top of a quiet, palm-lined street. My father had picked it for its view over the surrounding rooftops and, beyond, the placid diadem of the city. [...] At night you lay in bed and looked through the windows at the star-gleaming sky; you smelt the sun-baked earth, the sun-drenched foliage; you smelt the lemons, and the orange blossoms next door [...] (221-222)

Whereas the Maccaluccis and Simones do not reach "Paradise Valley" in *The Paesanos* story "Awinding We Did Go," the Simones in *Golden Wedding* seem very much to have arrived and settled in a paradise.

As the novel reaches its conclusion, Pagano condenses time with phrases such as "Five quickly fleeting years" (225) and "The four years that had elapsed" (262). Before Robert briefly recapitulates his parents' life, he states, "The history of their life was the history of an era, of a dozen eras" (284). And yet:

> In the world of my mother and father, these were not the events that mattered. The roll-call of the years conjured forth another tapestry—the

tapestry, spun of a million threads of blood, dream and desire, of bread, flesh and death, which was the history of their family. (285)

Family, state, and nation: *Golden Wedding* is an ethnic novel, an Italian American novel. It is also a Californian and an American novel. And it is a good one, too. Eureka! It is Pagano's gold.

Chapter 8

THE LITERATURE OF SPRAWL

Fiction writer Joseph Papaleo (1926-2004) wrote of the place and time he experienced: New York City, surrounding suburbs, and Italy from the 1930s until the latter part of the last century. In a long writing career stretching from the 1950s till the early years of the present century he published two novels (*All the Comforts* in 1967 and *Out of Place* in 1970) and one book of short stories (*Italian Stories* in 2002). Papaleo's fiction provides some understanding of how Italian Americans have looked at Italy as they experienced the alienation of a consumer culture. His fiction presents a mixed nostalgia for what Italy represents and recognition that it, too, like the United States, confronts continuous auto-dependent over-development. Papaleo grew up in the Bronx, served in the Air Force, and in 1946 became one of the first men to attend Sarah Lawrence College, graduating in 1949 twenty years before the college officially went co-ed. According to the *Sarah Lawrence Magazine*, Governor Thomas E. Dewey encouraged all of the state's colleges and universities to admit veterans, even Sarah Lawrence (8). Papaleo returned to Sarah Lawrence in 1960 as a professor, founded the Creative Writing program, and stayed until his retirement. Both his parents were born in Italy and like many Italian American authors, he wrote of the limits of assimilation and the pervasive, though evolving, nature of ethnic identity. However, Papaleo's fiction adds an additional geographical locus to his work, one beyond the Italian American standard of urban street or neighborhood, the post-World War II suburb. Furthermore, he adds an ethnic quotient to the predominantly Anglo-American literature of the suburbs.

The American suburb in the literature of the latter half of the twentieth century has been described by Catherine Jurca as a *"white diaspora*

[...] to emphasize and lay bare the role of the novel in promoting a fantasy of victimization" (8).[1] In the world of these fictions characters are "impoverished by prosperity" (7) and "the suburb and suburban house cheat characters out of the very thing that is supposed to be their white, middle-class, property-owning due" (5). Or, as the authors of *The Split-Level Trap* put it in 1960 (around the time Papaleo began to publish): "Having amassed a wealth that used to be the subject of fairy tales, he ['the typical American'] often finds that he isn't happy after all. Somewhere, something is missing" (20).

Contemporary social critics believed that the suburbs steal one's identity and homogenize too much. As an undergraduate Papaleo satirized in *The Campus*, the Sarah Lawrence student newspaper, the current American pressure to conform. In an April 1949 issue he poked fun at the Red Scare and the FBI. He wrote:

> Individuals purchasing peppers at markets and vegetable stores were followed to their homes and watched carefully. By the use of a sensitive wire-tapping device, agents were able to detect the distinct sound of a slice of pepper falling into a salad bowl. Those discovered "dropping the pepper", as the term came to be known, were apprehended. ("Browlined" 2)

If Papaleo's reference to vegetables, particularly peppers, gives his satire an Italian American ethnic flavor, his reference to "a radio-cinematic brave new world" in another brief essay from *The Campus* shows that he

---

[1] At the same time that insured mortgages "denied most racial minorities access not only to suburbia but also to the many benefits of homeownership," according to Freund, "[...] federal public housing, urban renewal, and highway programs undermined existing—often vibrant—minority communities in cities nationwide" (11). The most egregious example of racial residential segregation probably occurred in Detroit in 1941 when a private developer, though with the tacit approval of the Federal Housing Authority, built a concrete wall to keep races apart. American leaders were quick to condemn the Berlin Wall, but silent regarding the Detroit Wall. One kept Communist separate from Capitalist; the other kept black separate from white and while the Berlin Wall has been torn down, here in America we are still putting up Detroit Walls. Consider the exponential growth in gated communities.

dreaded the power of popular culture to homogenize American society. In this column he suggested a duel to the death between radio and film. "With luck," he wrote, "the two may eventually succeed in battering each other to a timely death" ("Joe Papaleo Discovers").

Papaleo's years as a soldier and student parallel those of the protagonist in Sloan Wilson's seminal suburban novel *The Man in the Grey Flannel Suit* (1955). Tom Rath, the protagonist, realizes late in the novel:

> I really don't know what I was looking for when I got back from the war, but it seemed as though all I could see was a lot of bright young men in grey flannel suits rushing around New York in a frantic parade to nowhere. They seemed to me to be pursuing neither ideals nor happiness—they were pursuing a routine. For a long while I thought I was on the side lines watching that parade, and it was quite a shock to glance down and see I too was wearing a grey flannel suit. (284)

Although most of Papaleo's stories and his novels appeared well-after the publication of Wilson's famous novel, the sort of self-realization noted in the above cited quotation typifies exactly the situation in all of Papaleo's fiction. In the 1970 novel *Out of Place* Gene Santoro, like a 1950s suburbanite, rushes around "in a frantic parade to nowhere" and pursues "neither ideals nor happiness." But in Papaleo's novel there is one important difference: Italy offers an escape—or the illusion of one —from deadening routine. Gene Santoro believed he could find his true place in the world and forsake gross American materialism by relocation to the old country. Yet, once he gets there, he acts like the archetypal suburbanite: driving and shopping.

In Italian American literature America has often been portrayed as a place of material prosperity but of little moral or spiritual integrity. Helen Barolini's *Umbertina*, for example, explores these differences. Near her death Umbertina imagines an old friend, Domenico, speaking to her: "'You call this success, Tinuzza, but in Italy there's a different *benessere* and the word is more gracious, not so materialistic. Well-being of the total person—not just money, but the spirit, too'" (145). And for

Umbertina's children and grandchildren real happiness, similar to postwar "suburban" instead of "ethnic" fiction, gets lost in the rush to accumulate things and more things. "Fires of understanding and affection never glowed" in the household of the next generation and "for all their material well-being, a vague despair stuck to them like a low-temperature contagion" (153). Umbertina's grand-daughter Marguerite wonders "where could she find happiness?" (153). Marguerite is one of many Italian American characters (or authors) who seek a sense of authenticity and purpose in Italy.

"My giant goes with me wherever I go," Emerson warned: "Our first journeys discover to us the indifference of places" ("Self-Reliance" 198). Rather than see oneself reflected back in the mirror of another culture, might it instead be said that there is only one mirror, that the giant *greets us wherever we go* and that giant is the United States? At the end of Barolini's most recent book, a study of Anglo American women in Italy, she bemoans changes in Italy. Everywhere she goes in Italy, she says, "Consumerism has adopted English as its language of choice: a supermarket calls itself 'Shopping Paradise'; a sign on an apartment building announced an 'Open House'—a new concept for Rome real estate" (*Their Other Side* 275). Italians, she says, are happy with the change while "we" "regret it" (285). Highways and construction cranes are everywhere. "There is nothing to do about the invasion of the new barbarians: Starbucks has embarked on bringing 'actual coffee' to the land of the *refined* espresso" (286).

Is this nostalgia for a world lost but another example of what Jurca calls "impoverishment by prosperity"? Italian American authors have often had an odd, romanticized, and inaccurate picture of the ancestral land. As noted in the chapter on John Fante's image of Italy, from Antonio Mangano in 1907 to Maria Laurino in 1996 many Italian American authors have journeyed to Italy and expressed joy and infatuation with Rome, but despair and disappointment with the village of parents, grandparents, or great-grandparents' birth. The American author never finds what he or she sought and usually despises the village. It never lives up to a romanticized vision and in actuality seems medieval. Today the Italian American author might be disturbed by the Starbucks in the town rather than the goat in the room.

Louise DeSalvo, for example, describes in *Crazy in the Kitchen* her return to a Southern Italian ancestral town. "It looks like Union City [New Jersey]," she says (173) and she adds, noting that this is the place her father believed to be "beautiful," it was in fact "the ugliest place I have ever seen in Italy" (178).

"The world has shrunk," Barolini writes at the end of *Their Other Side*, "and everything, everyplace, seems Americanized, not only in Italy" (286). Has the presence of the American giant been felt for much longer than the last decade? Could Gene Santoro in 1970 escape the suburban graveyard (Papaleo used this phrase in both the novel and in several short stories) by way of the Italian peninsula? The authors of *The Split-Level Trap* (1960) noted parenthetically that, "Europeans scoff at us for the hurry and worry in our lives (not realizing that they are traveling the same road themselves, a short way behind us)" (21).

In the mid-1960s novel *A Single Man* Christopher Isherwood describes at several points the evils of sprawl. For example, George, the protagonist, goes for a drive in his car in order to relax. (For Gene Santoro, driving was his "crowning pleasure of a day" [250].) George bemoans the encroachment of new houses in the Los Angeles hills. "True," Isherwood writes, "there are still a few uninhabited canyons, but George can't rejoice in them; he is oppressed by awareness of the city below. On both sides of the hills, to the north and to the south, it has spawned and spread itself over the entire plain" (111). George believes that, "it will die of overextension [...] brashness and greed [...] have been its only strength" (111). Yet, George, an expatriate Englishman teaching English literature at a Southern California state university, cannot return to his homeland to escape greed and sprawl. He has dinner with his friend Charlotte and she asks if he misses England. He thinks, "'Everything 's changed, and yet nothing has'" (131). He was born in a house built in 1649, but the current owner is "'a television producer in Manchester'" and the "'rebuilt'" interior now has central heating (132-133). When one looks out the back of the house one can still see the moors, but in front "'it's almost suburban [...] with buses running every twenty minutes into Manchester'" (133). The American giant casts its shadow far from Los Angeles and New York and because it does so George cannot go home again nor can Gene Santoro, as we will see, escape to Rome or Naples.

Italians, Barolini says in *Their Other Side*, "swell with pride as their country has passed from an agricultural society of the picturesque peasant with oxen and burro to become a major industrial nation of the world" (285). But this pride predates the Berlusconi era. Consider Italo Calvino's 1963 book *Marcovaldo*. The author indicates that the first group of stories "were written in the early 1950s and thus are set in a very poor Italy" while "the last stories date from the mid-60s, when the illusions of an economic boom flourished" (*Author's note*). Calvino satirizes the new Italy. In the first story in the collection Marcovaldo discovers mushrooms growing near his tram stop. This is a miracle for such a poor man who can barely earn enough to feed his family. "To Marcovaldo the gray and wretched world surrounding him seemed suddenly generous with hidden riches [...]" (2). By the end of the book Marcovaldo's city has been transformed—both in image and fact for Calvino speaks of skyscrapers, condominiums, and movie-theaters as well as "the sensation of material goods flowing on all sides [...]" (113). In this new city, "All during the day the big occupation of the productive public was to produce: they produced consumer goods. At a certain hour, as if a switch had been thrown, they stopped production and, away!, they were all off, to consume" (84). My point is that the *benessere* of the spirit, *pace* Domenico in *Umbertina*, may no longer exist just as George's house in England no longer sits in rural lands.

Papaleo's early novella "Arete" published in *The Dial* (1960) discusses the American influence on Italians. The main character, Gianni, is an Italian American staying in Italy with his friend Renato, an Italian ex-race car driver. Renato has married and become a family man. Papaleo writes, "Renato wanted to know the ways of American life because he, like his friends, looked towards America for cues. Italy had never before had a class like this—men who made their small wealth since the war [...]" (7). Renato wants to join the post-war middle-class. He plans one last car race to spread his name and hence secure his ownership of a new car dealership. His wife tells Gianni, "We have enough now'" and she asks him, "'what do you think is enough for a man? A house, a wife, children, a good living?'" (17). But that is the old Italy of the spirit. Renato seeks the new Italy of ownership. The story does not have a happy end: Renato crashes and dies.

Whether in Los Angeles, New York, Bologna, Rome or Naples the stories Isherwood, Calvino, and Papleo tell are ones that include poorly planned urban and suburban growth and ever-increasing motor-vehicular traffic; in other words, this is the literature of sprawl. "Sprawl," according to Harvard urban design and planning professor Alex Krieger, "though not literally synonymous with suburbanization, generally refers to suburban-style, auto-dominated, zoned-by-use development spread thinly over a large territory, especially in an 'untidy' or 'irregular' way" (45). Krieger identifies five main criticisms of sprawl and these are, I would add, similar to the complaints against suburbia that Jurca explains in *White Diaspora*: sprawl looks bad, it fosters conformity, it ruins the environment, it is dull, and, lastly, the not in my back yard attitude paradoxically perpetuates sprawl (46-49). Whereas Krieger meant his analysis to apply to North America, other scholars have noted "Euro-sprawl." "Europe," Alex Marshall has written, "has experienced its own urban exodus and suburbanization" (92). "Basically," he says "everything designed after World War II in the United States and in Western Europe looks and feels the same" (95). "Sprawl," according to Robert Bruegmann, "has been as evident in Europe as in America and can now be said to be the preferred settlement pattern everywhere in the world there is a certain measure of affluence and where citizens have some choice in how they live" (17). Bruegmann states that since 1970 Europe has seen "a quickening of the pace of suburban and exurban development, a sharp rise in automobile ownership and use, and the proliferation of subdivisions of single-family houses and suburban shopping centers" (199).

What this means for the Italian American author or an Italian American character in one of these author's books (or both) is that whereas in the past the author could not go to the ancestral home because of its poverty and primitiveness now there can be no return because of prosperity and global trends of convergence. My Coca-Cola goes with me wherever I go. In the streets of Naples the last remaining *banco dell' acqua* prepares no *spremuta* but sells the familiar red and white can—chilled and later I drive the high-speed by-pass highway built in 1975.

At the end of his recent book *Leaving Little Italy*, Fred Gardaphé mourns, "In their destruction, their transformations from Italian enclaves to gentrified hot spots, Little Italys have become little more than Italian theme parks that no longer resemble today's Big Italy" (154). Perhaps that is precisely how they *do* resemble Big Italy. Italy is also a theme park, just one of the many top destinations on the theme park planet. Even in 1970 as Gene Santoro travels in and around Naples and Amalfi he engages primarily in two activities: consumerism and driving. He does not spend his days in deep study of Benedetto Croce nor in the harvesting of Gragnano grapes. In Italy and the United States both the rural and the urban have been suburbanized.

Convergence from the 1960s to the present might be offered as an accurate depiction of Italian and American reality. Remo Bodei has written about the impact of automobiles, consumerism, and television on Italian culture. In his book *We, the Divided: Ethos, Politics and Culture in Post-War Italy, 1943-2006*, he says that politics has become completely dependent on the televised image and furthermore television "has led many people to replace direct and more interpersonal relationships with solitary afternoons and evenings in front of the small screen" (152). Again, that spiritual *benessere* that Umbertina's friend Domenico praised has disappeared, perhaps beneath the impervious surfaces of highway paving. Bodei claims that as early as the 1950s "the automobile outflanked the scooter in many families and began to replace the train as a means of transportation" (72). Besides creating the need for exponential growth of highways (as in the United States) in a manner similar to television the auto altered basic communal qualities of Italian life: "The automobile changed the way of life, forms of socialization and perceptions of distances and intimacy in Italy" (72). By the early 1960s, Bodei writes, "the ethics of consumption" surpassed "that of production" (92).

So it was for the American male caught in "the split-level trap" or in Papaleo's fiction. Yet, Papaleo's Italian characters want what his Italian American characters already have obtained: ownership of a piece of prosperity's pie. Renato in "Arete" wants his new car dealership and Carlo in *Out of Place* wants to own his own bakery, rather than work for others. In Papaleo's fiction and in *The Split-Level Trap* prosperity leads to despair. A typical scenario, according to Gordon, Gordon, and Gunther, "is that of a man who has succeeded and found that this was not what he wanted after all. He has all the money he needs; he has outdone his friends in climb, house and Cadillacs. Yet his life is stale and empty" (167). Papaleo worries in one of his poems, "History Lessons for Friday," that the immigrant groups to America after the Italians will also lose their *benessere* to dominant culture materialism.

> The Puerto Rican girls are blonde already,
> having given up their darkness of good frescoes
> to look like what they were told they should
> to get ahead, avoid being overlooked.

And if they succeed at being noticed and if they get ahead, then "they lose their bodies" and "they lose their souls."

In a novel fragment dated "ca. 1979" called "The Tony Chapter" Papaleo explores assimilation and stereotypes through a dialogue between different characters named Tony. The pop-singer Tony says, "'When you're on top, you're completely white and clean'" (5). He gets angry at one point and declares, "'I am no organ grinder for the people. I left all that behind in South Philly'" (6). Tony the senator says, "'There is—

and let me repeat this—there is *no* ethnicity anymore. I need not tell you about the melting pot, about pluralism and all that. Ethnic images were a fashion of the early [twentieth] century [...]'" (6). But senator Tony despairs the loss of ethnic traits and the gain of material comfort: we, he says, "turned ourselves inside out and shrank ourselves into nothing and gave our children the inferiority of conformity and the lowest horizon we could find—money'" (8).

Such loss of integral identity that succumbs to tempter America exists far from the siren torch of liberty's statue. Consider Gene Santoro's Italian brother-in-law Carlo. Unlike Renato in "Arete," Carlo in *Out of Place* does secure ownership of his own business in the new Italy (mainly through *American* Gene's financing). And when he does so, Carlo specializes in American pies. They are a big hit with tourists on the Amalfi coast and Carlo even plans to expand his market into Naples. He succeeds via clever marketing, not age old baking traditions. "What had worked so well was the idea of charging a high price, quite beyond reality, making the new also rare." The strategy works so well that Carlo watches the crowd of consumers "from the back of the shop, like a thief, seeing them accept the prices as if they alone proved quality." Then Papaleo adds the punch-line: "Even the Italians" (111).

Papaleo's final book *Italian Stories* moves in chronological order from a Bronx Italian neighborhood during the 1930s through a 1960s suburban diaspora to more recent times and Italian Americans who have moved in myriad directions, from Palm Springs, California to Florence, Italy. In addition to a "Prologue for an Ethnic Life," *Italian Stories* has twenty-six stories gathered from Papaleo's career and divided here into three sections. The stories of the first part take place in a Bronx Italian neighborhood during the 1930s—a neighborhood that had been abandoned by German and Irish residents before the Italians moved there.

The stories of the second section take place in the 1960s and the characters in these tales have moved away from the old neighborhood. An elderly man in "The End" remarks:

Did you ever see the streets of this neighborhood in the daytime? I never knew what it was in the years I worked. It's like a cemetery on these streets. I know. I walk it now. And yesterday I said to myself, what did we do, work our ass off to get out of the Bronx so we could live in a cemetery? (138-139)

The town he refers to in this passage is Scarsdale, a town often seen as the apotheosis of American desires.

The third group of stories begins with tales situated in the 1970s and continues to the near present. These stories develop the exploration of Italian American themes that run throughout the collection such as old world versus new world conflicts that result in confrontations between different generations of families that struggle to maintain a sense of solidarity.

Many of the stories throughout the book are auto-reliant. For example, in the final story of the first section, "Resting Place," an old priest and the members of a bereaved family ride in a limousine from the city to "a tree-encircled" suburban cemetery (101). Even death has moved to Westchester County. In the story "The End," from the second section, Angelo, a man who created a chain of food stores in Westchester, drives to the beach, sits in his car, and watches young men and women frolic in the sun. This is how he alleviates his sense of emptiness after his second heart attack. While he has achieved financial success, he feels that he has "never lived" (141) and wishes "he were dead" (144). In "Sizes," from the third section, the story revolves around a father's discussion with his daughter regarding what car she should purchase. Mr. Polero's driveway already has a line of cars: Mrs. Polero's "large Cadillac," Mr. Polero's "big Mercedes," Johnny's Camero (274), and soon a fourth car, one for each member of the household.

The protagonist of another third section story, "Memories Reflected in Palm Springs," has moved to the West coast not only for a successful career in the film industry, but also to "escape" (258) the constrictions of his East coast Italian American family. In California Frankie tries to assimilate via geography and a swimming pool (topography), but like Gene in *Out of Place*, a parent calls him home. Frankie recalls the old neighborhood, "The hallways that hold smells forever and light-bulbs behind glass covers that collect oily dust" (260). He is a successful art director and set designer for films with a young starlet wife and yet he asks himself, "What did I want?" (264). He goes back to New York for his father's death and funeral and when he returns to California, Frankie and his wife Annie go for a drive along Mulholland. They stop to look at the view:

> I begin to cry as I watch it. I don't know why? The vastness? The lines of light go as far as Bakersfield. But it is the vastness from here, and I think of my father whirled out of his easy Bronx bed into space where the other millions are all on a trip, not knowing which way to go. (265)

Everyone moves out and drives on a trip to some unknown, everyone in life or in death to Westchester or California or even, as Gene Santoro, to Naples, Italy.

Out of Place, a novel in three parts, begins in the New York metropolitan area. Gene's brother-in-law, Carlo, now separated from his wife Anna, has taken his children, Carlino and Joanna, to Italy. Gene, an Italian American success story, the eldest, wealthiest, and most accomplished child of Francesco Santoro, has been chosen to rescue Carlino and Joanna. Gene travels to Italy, has an extramarital affair with Carlo's young housekeeper and needlessly prolongs his stay, but eventually he returns to the United States with his nephew and niece. Meanwhile, his father has purchased a house-as-fortress where all the Santoros can live together. Gene and his wife Francine refuse to do so.

Part two of the novel takes place in Westchester County and New York City. Gene interacts with his wife and with his brother, Angelo, as well as his sister and father. His father becomes more demanding and Gene sometimes comes to the house-as-fortress to spring his nephew and niece. Mostly, he takes them for rides in his car.

Carlino and Joanna practically disappear from the third section. Gene returns to Southern Italy. He attends Carlo's wedding, meets Carlo's young relative Bianca and has an extended affair with her. He may have fathered a child with Carlo's former housekeeper, Elena, who is now married, but living further south.[2] Bianca and Gene visit Elena, and then Bianca and Gene move to Rome. The binds of family reach far and Carlo comes to Rome to tell Gene that he must hurry home to New York, for Gene's father is dying. Unlike Frankie in the later story "Memories Reflected in Palm Springs," Gene gets home too late to see his father one last time. Gene patches things up with his siblings, his wife, and his two sons, who appear in the novel for the first time. Gene and Francine will move to Rome and the two boys will visit while on break from prep school.

Buying and driving are everywhere in the novel, with little differentiation between Naples and New York. Gene's American giant does indeed travel with him wherever he goes. He conducts his search for inner peace and harmony in a car on a highway and with a wallet ever-full of cash. Yet, Gene boasts to Francine after his first trip that in Italy "'life is going on outside; they're all so different from each other; everybody you meet has a little crack to make, his eyes are open, nothing's locked up, nothing's locked up [...]'" (96), while at "the fort" in Westchester "the rooms separated from each other the way Americans were" (132). Gene, with his constant driving and buying, however, carries the American separateness with him wherever he goes. In Amalfi, he does not become a man of the people, a man who as he tells Francine at the novel's conclusion can tell "the difference between flesh and blood and ants" (258). He spends. He even buys Carlo a yellow Fiat 850 for a wedding present.

Papaleo sought to idealize Southern Italy, to offer it as an escape for the stressed out middle-aged Italian American professional, but Papa-

---

[2] In Wilson's *Man in a Grey Flannel Suit*, protagonist Tom Rath discovers that he had fathered a love child in Rome near the end of the Second World War. Both Rath and Santoro engage the American solution: send money.

leo's words undercut such a depiction. For example, descriptions of Naples near the start of the book mirror descriptions of the Bronx at the end of the second section. When Gene arrives in Naples the first time he doesn't like it at first. Then he gets a haircut and buys some clothes and then miraculously feels better than he ever has in his life. It wasn't a vision of the Madonna, nor a hike in the hills that caused such a shift: it was cash.

When Gene sits down with Carlo to discuss the fate of the children, Carlo defends their life in Italy by claiming Carlino and Joanna had no life in America: "'Are they children over there, driven to stores, walking through stores? Objects!'" (36). The children's life in the Mezzogiorno doesn't seem that different from their life in Westchester. When Gene takes the children with him to Naples, he defends Naples after Carlino complains of the smell as they approach the city: "'It's only these oil plants at the end of town. Like New Jersey. You remember the smell just when you start on the turnpike'" (45). And when they finally park the car and get out, Gene takes his charges to stores and buys them sneakers, toys; "a peasant doll, which had an American face [...]" (45). Gene spends wildly, surprised by the variety and quality of the available merchandise. On another auto trip, Gene tries to point out some sights to the children as they speed along the highway to Rome but gives up for "they were not looking: their faces were on the toys, as if on a family ride along the Bronx River Parkway" (69).

And when they return to New York they do the same exact thing: Gene takes them for rides and buys them things. They do, in fact, drive along the Bronx River Parkway: "driving was like escaping" (106). They stop on one such trip at Korvette and, "Inside the store, the children were excited: the filled shelves were a welcome Amalfi did not have, the swollen fullness that took away fear" (106). In Amalfi one felt empty due to a lack of consumer goods (though there seems little difference in range of goods as presented in the novel) and in America one felt empty due to the lack of human interaction (though, again, there seems no distinction in characters' *actions* in one place or the other).

When Gene returns to Italy and meets Bianca they discuss the differences and similarities between Italy and America. Bianca claims that Americans either buy or "'kill everything. We are all yours now,'" she says, "'and you know it'" (215). Then she surprises Gene by telling him nonetheless "'I would be ready to try it'," the United States (215). She explains, "'Because the place is full of things I want to buy'" (215). Gene then, who "had thought conversations here would go away from the office, and from money" (215), tells Bianca he could get her a job in New York and then he realizes that here in Amalfi, too, "the candy America, the great store, the dollar shower; it was what he had to boast about instead of monuments and towns like Amalfi" (215). His American giant travels with him wherever he goes, the shadow the giant casts disallows clear sight of the place where Gene stands and, hence, in Italy as in America, Gene is "out of place."

One difference between the alienated affluence of Tom Rath in *The Man in the Grey Flannel Suit* and Gene Santoro is that Rath belongs to mainstream old money culture. Ethnic difference must be considered in any examination of Santoro's suburban angst. At times Gene pines for the old days in the immigrant neighborhood and at other times he praises his dad, a successful button manufacturer, for getting them out of there. He worries that the very word "Westchester" means "a thorough whitewash, skin and hair becoming lighter" (20). Indeed, Gene shares Carlo's opinion of American women. Carlo tells Carla shortly before their marriage when she asks him if he has a wife in America: "'There are no wives in America. Only drivers of cars, models for washing machines and cigarettes. No flesh and blood [...] In every house a Doris Day'" (117). Similarly, Gene criticizes Francine when he has returned to the United States for dieing her hair blonde (261), though the fact that his two prep-school sons are "taller, lighter than the family" and move and speak in an "old Connecticut" manner does not perturb him (267). Gene tells Francine, something Tom Rath never says to his wife Betsy, that they never really liked the suburbs, "'this dead place with empty streets'" (259), *because* their neighbors—the Raths, let's say—never liked them: the Santoros, Gene says, are "'too *dark* for" the suburbs (259). Gene continues, "We're second-rate around here. Too short and too dark and we got too much black hair and we're too heavy-set [...]'" (261). Maybe Westchester will like Gene and Francine's two sons. But neither Gene nor Carlo nor Papaleo himself seem to see any of the contradictions here. Carlo says of American women, "'Machines are them; they are the machines; what were women',," he says, "'are now handles, parts for the machine. And worse. Worse. They like it'" (117). But of the customers who crowd Carlo's bakery *in Amalfi* for American pies priced ridiculously high, Papaleo notes, they all like it: "Even the Italians" (111).

The late Jean Baudrillard claimed "it is Disneyland that is authentic" in America (104). If so, then it is Disneyworld that is authentic on planet Earth. Whereas Baudrillard saw "an unbridgeable rift" (73) between America and Europe, I have proposed an indelible and unshakable connectivity. In the debate regarding the continuing significance of the local and the omnipotent presence of the global, I have observed here the latter.[3] And in this globalized world of convergence, is everyone paradoxically "out of place" everywhere? Is everyone a migrant? "Migrants," Graziella Parati has written, "experience a double absence: absent as they are from their country of origin and a familiar culture and pushed into a position of erasure and expendability at the margins of the country of immigration" (25). Italy is a destination culture, a promised

---

[3] The planning challenges facing Westchester County are similar to those confronting other metropolitan areas within the nation and across the globe. This fact became very clear to me during two recent trips: one to Portland, Maine and the other to Naples, Italy. Consider that paragon of New England planning ever held up to shame the mayors of lesser towns—Portland, a small city steadily losing population and trying to survive on tourism. Yet, the surface parking lots that those tourists require blight the cityscape. As my airplane made its descent into Naples—that "vast ecosystem crackling with tenor horns and basso transmissions" (83) as contemporary Italian American novelist John Domini has described it, I saw a desolate medieval castle on a barren hillside. Then I saw an IKEA surrounded by its moat of tar, drawbridge down and lot full to bursting.

land for the early twenty first-century as America was for the early twentieth-century. Now in both countries there are destination suburbs, exclusionary places of affluence and sprawl. Papaleo wrestled with his identity both as a writer and an ethnic American. He was "out of place" and struggled to find a niche between suburb and city and between glossy New York fiction-writing and something more adventuresome. The convergences in his world and in his life may very well have been the root of a new alienation.

Chapter 9

THE BLACK HAND BECOMES THE BIG BOX

It has been more than fifteen years since a Wal-Mart opened near the famous Ninth Street Italian Market in Philadelphia. What bit of Philadelphia's "Little Italy" that remains—like those of other cities—may no longer be a cohesive ethnic neighborhood, but now a manufactured spectacle. A "Little Italy" as tourist site does not represent resistance to globalization, but contrarily acquiesces to it and typifies it in that such sites are exemplars of what Guy Debord has called "the society of the spectacle." In his book of the same title Debord has written: "the spectacle corresponds to the historical moment at which the commodity completes its colonization of social life. It is not just that relationship to commodities is now plain to see—commodities are now *all* that there is to see [...]" (29). The South Philadelphia we see today is the world of Wal-Mart, plus the cheese steak sandwich.

The poetry of two Philadelphia poets, Frank S. Spiziri, an early twentieth-century cobbler, and J. T. Barbarese, a present day professor, demonstrates that both the immigrant's and the grandchild of immigrants' poetry can resist assimilation and homogenization. If viewed from the Debordian perspective, such resistance is not possible in the present because, as Debord has said, "there is no place left where people can discuss the realities which concern them" (*Comments* 19) and, it would follow, there is no place left for Italian Americans in this particular locale, Philadelphia, because its Little Italy has been transformed by media and merchandising into a would-be all powerful spectacle. If in the early twentieth-century the Black Hand threatened to pull the community apart from within, now it is possible to blame a new mythological monster: the big box. Yet, community continues, though in different ways. In fact, the poet of today must leave the commodified Little Italy in order to sustain an Italian American poetic just as the poet of yesteryear had to leave impoverished Italy in order to sustain life.

Frank S. Spiziri, born in 1878, left the hillside town of Corigliano Calabro around 1895 and, after nine years in New York, moved with his parents and siblings to Philadelphia. When the Spiziri family moved to Philadelphia they found an established Italian neighborhood. "By the 1860 federal census," sociologist Richard N. Juliani has noted, "Italians for the first time manifested a significant clustering of population in the southeast quarter of the newly expanded city, a precursor of the huge concentration that settled in that area in subsequent years" (*Building Little Italy* 301). According to Juliani, "they became macaroni manufactures, grocers, wine importers, and tavern keepers" (301), and these commercial enterprises marked this part of town as "the 'Italian quarter'" (302). This concentration and its visibility increased steadily even prior to the decades of peak immigration.

Between the year of J. T. Barbarese's birth, 1948, and Frank Spiziri's death, 1958, Philadelphia as a whole and its Italian neighborhood in particular began to change. After 1950 Philadelphia began to lose manufacturing jobs while the number of jobs available in the surrounding suburbs increased, and so Italian Americans moved there. Indeed, the Italian American neighborhood had disproportionate population loss. Juliani has stated that, "during a forty year interval, while the total population of the city had fallen about 23%, the reduction of South Philadelphia was about 45%" ("Community and Identity" 51).

And then along came Wal-Mart. It did not come alone. Juliani has recalled, "In June 1994 a devastating fire destroyed Palumbo's, once a boarding house for newly arrived immigrants, and more recently a popular restaurant that reflected the continuity of the Italian presence in South Philadelphia longer than any other commercial establishment" ("Community and Identity" 46). A corporate chain drug store replaced it. Near the end of the year 1994, Juliani added, "after more than 70 years of providing customers with Italian cookies and cakes, Joseph Termini, the owner of the best known pastry shop in the neighborhood, died" (46). Juliani has stated that after this death and fire, "the control of retail stores crucial to community life [...] is shifting from individuals and families who themselves are local residents to massive national corporations, such as Wal-Mart, who seem to voraciously devour small businesses, sidewalks and neighborhoods" ("Community and Identity" 53). And so Juliani has concluded "that the community that began more than a century ago as an immigrant colony before evolving into the ethnic neighborhood of more recent years is now reaching its final stage" ("Community and Identity" 47).

J. T. Barbarese concurs. He told me: "The neighborhood structure is altered completely. More bars, big stop-&-shop complexes. Smith Playground, where I played base- and basketball as a teenager, is overgrown with weeds, backstops in poor condition." He added, "The second floor pool halls, like Mosconi's, the bakeries and dollar stores were infinitely preferable to the more streamlined commodified alternatives" (email correspondence 13 April 2004).

Frank Spiziri did not leave this neighborhood once he got there. Amazingly, however, in his poems he never mentioned it. Instead, he looked back to Italy, as Barbarese, at times, looks back to the ethnic enclave of his youth. In other words, both poets look back, though to different locales and times. For both poets, as Giacomo Leopardi said, "Remembrance is fundamental and of first importance in poetic feeling" (93). If estrangement has become a normal condition of modern life, then memory may be a possible therapy as well as or instead of a disciplinary strap or imaginative fantasy.

Frank Spiziri's granddaughter, the well-known scholar of American religious history Catherine Albanese, has translated her grandfather's poems and published them in a volume entitled *A Cobbler's Universe* (1997). Introducing the work she notes that her grandfather wrote poems "in two series with a wide span of years dividing them. The early poems were all apparently written from February 1917 to July 1918, a period of eighteen months. And after a literary silence of seventeen years, the later poems were composed over a three-and-one-half year period between 1935 and 1938" (91). He wrote the poems, Albanese speculates, to demonstrate the uniqueness of the immigrant Spiziri family and to project a certain image of his status in particular. "For him," Albanese says, "middle-class status continued to be an issue as he struggled to attain the social place in which he felt he belonged" (39). He believed, according to his granddaughter, that through his poetry "the rank he secured would surely reflect on family honor" (42). But the status and honor he sought did not mean to reach the city at large but just the Italian neighborhood where, Albanese recalls, he strolled in "a derby hat and then Borselino felt" and where "he carried a Boston bag— containing only his lunch and cobbler's apron—that led neighbors to call him 'the doctor'" (42).

Since neighborhood status and honor concerned him, it was to his neighbors that he presented his poems. "His gift poems," according to Albanese, "linked him effectually to others, and [...] at the same time [...]" created "obligation and" assured "a social return" (90). Emerson said that "a man's biography is conveyed in his gifts" ("Gifts" 376) and Spiziri's gifts, his poetry "reveals" -- in the words of his granddaughter -- "a man *in* but not *of* America" (56). Not only does his poetry look back to Italy, it is often pastoral. In other words, Spiziri wrote in a city in America, but wrote of a rural landscape in a distant country that he knew only as a boy. For example, in one early poem, "Heartfelt," he wrote:

> Over there,
> In the middle of the olive trees,
> In a little white house,
> Hidden from others' eyes,
> There we will move in,
> There we will live happily (116)

And in the later group of poems he may have included philosophical and political as well as pastoral and romantic themes, but some of these he wrote in dialect, not in standard Italian as all his earlier poems. In the first poem that he signed with the Americanized spelling of his name (one *z* and one *r* instead of two), he wrote with nationalistic fervor for the home country:

> For bequeathed to us is the cult right and holy
> Of the ever-new fame of an ancient age,
> That does not diminish but continually increases,
> Returning us there where Rome first began.
> ("Father Superior" 145-146)

Although he sometimes signed the poems with his name, date, and the location "Philadelphia," he never wrote of his adopted home city. Instead, he entreated in one poem: "Turn back: fix your eye / Toward the Latin sky" ("[Birthday] Rememberings" 142). In the Italian community of South Philadelphia, Spiziri kept Italy present and in his multicultural community of present day Philadelphia J. T. Barbarese, as we will see, keeps Little Italy present.

In his essay "What is Italian-American Poetry," Dana Gioia has stated that, "each new generation of Italian-Americans finds its links with the old country more tenuous. As the Little Italies disappear, and families disperse to the suburbs, the descendants of Italian immigration gradually merge their once sharply differentiated ethnic identity in mainstream America" (167). There are limits to this merging: just as ethnic identity constantly shifts and evolves so too does the mainstream, sharp differentiation may continue. Identity does not depend solely on place and concentration of numbers. As many scholars have pointed out, a member of one generation may reject all things Italian in an urge to Americanize while a younger member of the same family may seek reconnection with all things Italian. Ethnicity is not necessarily linear. This is a central theme in Italian American literature, one that can be seen quite clearly in Helen Barolini's foundation work *Umbertina*. Furthermore one *can* carry one's *italianità* to Cherry Hill, New Jersey. Gioia has concluded, "The new generation of Italian-American intellectuals know as well as their immigrant grandparents did that assimilation is the easiest road to success" (174). Yet, in his poetry Barbarese, who Gioia in his former capacity as Poetry Editor of *Italian Americana* selected as his last featured poet, often notes the limits of assimilation and differentiates his world from that of Wal-Mart and Walgreens.

Guy Debord would have it: we "can never lastingly free" ourselves "from the crushing presence of media discourse and of the various forces organized to relay it" (*Comments* 19). Emerson long ago claimed that, "it is cold, lifeless business when you go to the shops to buy me something" ("Gifts" 376). Spiziri presented his poems to his neighbors as gifts. So, too, does J. T. Barbarese. It is our obligation, if we receive them, to hear what they record. I asked Joe Barbarese if his children speak fondly of a South Philadelphia that no longer exists or that is now a stage set at best. He replied, "They know nothing of it [...]" (email correspondence, 13 April 2004). Just as Spiziri kept Italy alive in the ethnic neighborhood of South Philadelphia and by doing so fostered community and resisted homogenization, so Joe Barbarese keeps Little Italy alive in multi-cultural America and by doing so forces us to question alienating forms of community created by a corporate culture that raids ethnicity for a patina of nostalgia.

Let us consider for a moment the work of Philadelphia's greatest artist of Italian American heritage, the architect Robert Venturi. In his first treatise, *Complexity and Contradiction in Architecture* (originally published in 1966), Venturi said, "as an architect I try to be guided not by habit but by a conscious sense of the past—by precedent, thoughtfully considered" (13) and this thoughtful consciousness has been paramount to his work for the more than forty years since. Yet, this has never meant that he has turned his back on the present. In fact, it is the intersection of past and present that inspires his art. In his first treatise he wrote:

> The consistent spatial order of the Piazza S. Marco, for example, is not without its violent contradictions in scale, rhythm, and textures, not to mention the varying heights and styles of the surrounding buildings. Is there not a similar validity to the vitality of Times Square in which the

jarring inconsistencies of buildings and billboards are contained within the consistent order of space itself? (54)

The "messy vitality" (16) that has so interested Venturi has its parallel in ethnicity in that "the jarring inconsistencies" of identity "are contained within" the consistent order of the body itself. Thus, in a recent Barbarese poem the speaker can mention Roy Orbison, Mozart, the Supremes, Hendrix, and Brahms and think while sitting in a Starbuck's:

> Pretty woman, talk to me
> *nel mezzo del camin',*
> tell me why you're here
> so I'll know why I am (*The Black Beach* 36)

This is just the sort of mixing of forms that has interested Venturi. Indeed, he may be both the prophet and the master of it. In his second treatise *Learning From Las Vegas* (1972), co-authored with Denise Scott Brown and Steven Izenour, the architects compare the triumphal arches in the Roman Forum to the billboards along Route 66. They asserted that, "spatial characteristics of form, position, and orientation are secondary to their symbolic function. Along the highway, advertising Tanya via graphics and anatomy, like advertising the victories of Constantine via inscriptions and bas-reliefs, is more important than identifying in space" (117). This can be said of the ethnic neighborhood as well—one can identify in more ways than just spatially.

In North Philadelphia many years ago Venturi and company designed a headquarters for the mid-Atlantic region catalogue store BASCO. They created a large box structure dominated by a large sign that brightly proclaimed BASCO. Of course, this is architecture for the car age. The car took Italian-Americans out of Little Italies and into the suburbs. As Barbarese wrote to me, "my generation having gone east (Cherry Hill, Deptford, Medford)" has left the city neighborhood (email correspondence, 13 April 2004). Yet, ethnic self-identification has survived. The dominance of the car, however, may now be a fact of yesteryear and so we meet not on the street corner but on the worldwide web screen. Venturi therefore has recently been promoting a digital architecture: "electronic sparkle," he has said, "can parallel the glitter of mosaics" ("Sweet and Sour" 51).

This postmodern ethnic optimism does not preclude complaint. J. T. Barbarese told me, "there's no escaping the rage, which grounds or grinds up imaginative desire, and I think only the children (and / or grandchildren) of the immigrant appreciate that or can feel its sting" (email correspondence 6 June 2004). In a recent poem entitled "Danielle" Barbarese describes a young rebellious student. The speaker of the poem tells us, "I last saw her a couple of years later / leaning on that night's guido / at the bar of the Trump Towers / nodding into the toot, the booze, and the noise [...]." But if Danielle's world seems confused, so, too, does the teacher's mainstream, proper world for "oafish fact" and "ugly accuracy" comprise it. Additionally, very bitter criticism of the lessons of assimilation and the American way can be found in "Our Father." The poem ends:

They preached the American gospel
of hard work means success

and the immigrant religion
whose eucharist was loot.
Life itself was stolen goods.
They're buried in stolen suits. (*A Very Small World* 24)

In an op-ed piece published in *The Philadelphia Inquirer*, Barbarese recalls being in a class as a teenager "filled with WASPs from the Main Line who ask the Polish kids if they know which end of their pencils to gnaw and the Italian Americans if they're allowed in the ocean" ("Lessons in Race"). Barbarese was one of the Italian kids, very much an outsider. Born in 1948, he is the grandson of immigrants, and the son of Joseph Anthony and Antoinette (D'Aniballe) Barbarese. J. T. (Joe) Barbarese lived in the South Philadelphia Italian neighborhood until his early twenties (email correspondence 13 April 2004). He left the neighborhood to attend Franklin and Marshall College and graduate school at Temple University. He taught English at Friends Select School in Center City Philadelphia and then moved to the English Department at Rutgers University, —Camden.

He may have left the old neighborhood many years ago, but he has not left the city, nor has he forsaken his Italian American identity. He now resides in Mt. Airy, a section of the Philadelphia known as a model for multi-cultural urban living. In his poetry, too, he has not left the city, and, on occasion, in his poetry he returns to the old neighborhood. *Under the Blue Moon,* his first book, contains thirty-eight poems and Barbarese identifies six of them as growing out of the old neighborhood (email correspondence, 13 April 2004). His second book, *New Science,* has fewer poems explicitly about the old neighborhood, but this does not establish a pattern for his two newest books both have several South Philadelphia / Italian American poems.

Even though J. T. Barbarese, the grandson of immigrants, has become a professor his work demonstrates resistance more than, as Gioia would have it, assimilation to mainstream America (both of his newest books contain poems very critical of recent US government policy). Barbarese told me that although he never felt "White" growing up, he also could never embrace "alienation as a part of American social conditioning because something else, imagination and desire, entered to 'rescue' (or delude)" him (email correspondence 6 June 2004). He has found sustenance and solace in a formalism that serves as a means to convey and assert self-expression. In introducing his featured poem in *Italian Americana,* he said, "Form is the body armor [...] of the assaulted sensibility" (187). Barbarese says no to the homogenized world. In addition to formalism, history functions as a means of opposition, not assimilation, to the mass-mediated world. "The essence of the contemporary lyric, I think," Barbarese conjectured in his introduction, "is the close call—instances that measure your size *in relation to history"* (187 italics mine).

One *Under the Blue Moon* poem, "Street Scene," opposes the real and the ideal and then ends with Old World determinism. "America," Barbarese writes in a *New Science* poem, "sticks to Americans' lives / like a brand name" ("Firewood Talk, 25 October 1983" 50) and in "Street Scene" the poet peels back the gummy label rich in promise of false reward. "Camelot" for these city youths was "a cardboard box" and in the urban park down by the refineries and factories "there were no deer" and "the horror: the stone dropped down the well / never clucked, never hit the side ever" (45).

Old South Philadelphia has a relatively new Wal-Mart but the shipyards and factories are gone. In 1981 Jerre Mangione reflected on his old Mount Allegro neighborhood, Rochester, New York. He noted: "gone are the clapboard houses with their front porches [...]" (287) and gone, too, are "the storytelling sessions [...] because television by then had reared its voracious head and seemingly swallowed their tongues" (301). But all has not been merged and lost, only changed. As Fred L. Gardaphé concludes near the end *Leaving Little Italy*, "Now that the great majority of Americans of Italian descent no longer live in Little Italys, it will be the job of culture, and not place, to help maintain and transmit a cultural identity that we can call Italian American" (152). This is one job that J. T. Barbarese fulfills with his poetry, but the identity he projects is never simple, unitary, or pre-given. "I'm not what they say I am / when they call me by a name / cobbled out of memory or / raked off the last generation / and some old lady's Bible," he states at the start of "Dawn," a poem *this* Joseph concludes, "Not the name they gave me, / not what the name says, / I add what I come on" (*Under the Blue Moon* 33).

Frank Spiziri, too, added what he "came on" in that he arrived in Philadelphia a trained cobbler, but added the designation "poet" to his name, his identity. He fashioned himself a gentleman and walked down the Philadelphia streets with Boston bag and Borsalino hat musing on the old country.

Does ethnicity need the urban village to exist? I think not. The possibility to discuss what concerns us still exists: if not on the street, then from our suburban gardens and out on the worldwide web. Barbarese has not written a Wal-Mart poem, but he has written a poem called "Inside Bradlee's Department Store." It opens: "I am exhausted by products, / by what and how many they are, / objects shedding their pasts like arriving immigrants." Our conversation about who we have been and who we are will continue and this conversation, in turn, will continue to shape our individual and group identity. Who we become may differ from who we have been and who we are, but still it may also be Italian American.

Chapter 10

Always Different

To metamorphose one's identity may necessitate transgressing boundaries such as gender expectation or neighborhood limits. And it may take force of will to defeat an imprisoning sense of fate. I have been a friend of the poet Elaine Equi for years. I never thought of her as an Italian American poet (I thought she was probably of French ancestry) until one day when I needed some information from the Poetry Society of America web site, I saw that Elaine had contributed a short essay there titled "What is American About American Poetry?" in which she says:

> Both my parents came to America from Italy in the 1920s, bringing with them very specific and old-fashioned ideas about what is acceptable behavior for men and for women. My whole life I've been acutely aware of these boundaries and struggled with crossing them.

Although Equi does not often write poems explicitly of ethnic content, when Equi left home for the big city—New York—she lived for the most part on Mulberry Street, once an Italian immigrant neighborhood. As she explained to me: "I have thought about what attracted me to Mulberry Street and all I can say is I just felt incredibly at home once I saw it" (email correspondence 14 September 2003).[1] When crossing some boundaries, others remain intact: one picks and chooses.

The boundaries transgressed by the author who foregrounds her ethnicity may be her other subject identities. So in the prologue to her memoir *Vertigo* Louise DeSalvo states:

---

[1] Elaine Equi has written a poem called "Mulberry Street." It appears on page 48 of *Decoy* (Minneapolis: Coffee House Press, 1994) and on page 136 of *Ripple Effect: New and Selected Poems* (Minneapolis: Coffee House Press, 2007).

> I am, inescapably, an Italian-American woman with origins in the working class. I come from a people who, even now, seriously distrust educated women, who value family loyalty. The story I want to tell is that of how I tried to create (and am still trying to create) a life that was different from the one that was scripted for me by my culture [...]. (xvii)

On the other hand, the boundaries transgressed by the author who foregrounds her aesthetic may be the limitations of genre. So for Elaine Equi, the boundary between a "populist impulse" and "the imagination in all its exotic plumage" is one that she tries to erase in her poetry. She relates this aesthetic impulse directly to her heritage. She says, "this is a dynamic I saw in my own home where there was often tension between wanting to achieve something, yet not wanting to appear to be 'putting on airs' or trying to be something you weren't" ("What Is American"). To cross genres or to leave the neighborhood requires the power necessary to overcome prescribed fate. Poetry was the fire that fueled Equi's journey. Virginia Woolf functioned in this way for DeSalvo: "She is English, purely and highly bred. I am more Italian than American, rough, tough, a street kid, out of a working-class neighborhood in Hoboken, New Jersey. We have nothing in common, except that we're both women, and that, I think, is enough" (*Vertigo* 239). DeSalvo's study of Woolf took her out of Hoboken, but through the community of women's writing she returned to her home, her past and saw it with a new lens, one that enabled her more recent memoir writing.

Louisa Ermelino's three novels—*Joey Dee Gets Wise* (1991), *The Black Madonna* (2001), and *The Sisters Mallone* (2002)—explore the blessings and curses of an ethnic neighborhood. In her fiction, the ethnic enclave is both a sanctuary and a trap, and many characters in her work seek to get out of the neighborhood. Her three novels move from male-centered (*Joey Dee*) to mother-son relationships (*The Black Madonna*) to the forging of a women's community (*The Sisters Mallone*). In the most recent novel, characters demonstrate the most skill in escaping suffocation in the urban village. The Mallone sisters are able to do this because of the many boundaries they are able to cross and the roles that they are able to assume. Ermelino's progression in these novels, from male centered to critique of male centered to women's community and the elimination of the male, illustrates the history of the Italian American woman writer.

Until recently, unlike African American, Irish American, or Jewish American women, there was no such thing as the classification Italian American women's writing. There were, of course, Italian American women authors, but the formulation of a community of writers, a tradition of writing, and scholars to study it is a recent conception. Mary Jo Bona titled her 1999 study, *Claiming a Tradition: Italian American Women Writers* with this fact very much in mind. Furthermore, one could argue that although an Italian American men's tradition of writing pre-dates that of Italian American women, all the institutional critical apparatus of tradition formation has been recently shaped despite the fact that important male writers such as Pietro di Donato, John Fante, and Jerre Mangione came of age in the 1930s. Consider that Edvige Giunta and Kathleen McCormick have recently published a Modern Language Association book titled *Teaching Italian American Literature, Film, and Popular Culture* while similar books in the areas of African, Native, and Asian American literature were published in the 1980s.

Many reasons account for the late appearance of an Italian American women's literary tradition. In addition to Bona, Edvige Giunta's *Writing with an Accent: Contemporary Italian American Women Authors* also explains the recent growth in this body of writing and celebrates the women who write it. One woman key to both Giunta and Bona is Helen Barolini, whose introduction to her 1985 *The Dream Book: An Anthology of Writings by Italian American Women* is the wellspring from which interpreters of this literature draw.

I would offer eight reasons for the recent surfacing of Italian American women's literary expression and its emerging codification as a tradition. First, like their male counterparts, early women immigrants had to devote all their energies to survival. Also, like their male counterparts, immigrant women often lived in insular communities that did not encourage language acquisition. Women's roles within the Italian American family and family loyalty also deterred literary expression. As DeSalvo and Giunta write in the introduction to their recent anthology *The Milk of Almonds: Italian American Women Writers on Food and Culture,* "The works presented here are written by women whose Italian American cultural heritage holds sacred the principle of silence and would prefer that the experiences of its members remain hidden, unexpressed" (13). Giunta notes in her study that "Women writers of Italian descent have to fight both the culture that silences their ethnicity and the ethnicity that silences their gender" (81).

Another factor that delayed the now burgeoning Italian American women's literary expression is this ethnicity's view of education. One component of this view is that education should be practical, not bookish, and another belief asserts that sons should be educated first, then daughters. DeSalvo in her memoir *Vertigo* describes "a bookcase filled with a set of books" in her house but adds that her father and mother did not read these books and "yet," she continues, "ours is the only parlor I know with books in it" (54). For both the Italian American man and woman a step into college, into literary culture, into self-expression is a step away from family and neighborhood and so Equi worried about "putting on airs."

When the Italian American first writes, she may write white or Anglo partly for acceptance in the dominant community. Louise DeSalvo wrote extensively about Virginia Woolf for many years, and Josephine Gattuso Hendin published a book on Flannery O'Connor long before she published a novel of her own. Because, until very recently, the idea of an Italian American women's tradition of writing did not exist, it has taken the conscious efforts of women such as Helen Barolini, Josephine Gattuso Hendin, and Louise DeSalvo to develop a readership. In 1985 Barolini noted:

> The Italian American woman writer seems to have been stranded in a no-woman's land where there was small choice: either follow the omnipresent models that do not speak her own particular experience, or write of her

experience and know that it will be treated as of no importance, "too different" for critical attention. (31)

Even as recently as 2002, DeSalvo and Giunta asserted in the introduction of their anthology: "There is, in the culture of the United States, no general recognition that a tradition of Italian American women's literature exists" (13). Bona is correct: this is a time for "claiming a tradition."

Without a tradition there can be no models for younger women authors and, therefore, less possibility for self-validation. "As a working-class girl, born and raised in Hoboken, New Jersey," DeSalvo writes, "how could I hope to fulfill a life's ambition, to do serious intellectual work, to become a critic, and writer? [...] I had no role model among the women of my background to urge me on [...]" (*Vertigo* 9). A decade before Barolini said: "Italian American women had long been denied the possibility of finding themselves in literature. How could they affirm an identity without becoming familiar with the models by which to perceive themselves?" ("Introduction" 28).

This leads to brief mention of the final deterrent to the establishment of an Italian American women's literary tradition: the marketplace. Often, it seems that the success or failure of a literary work has nothing to do with its quality, but hinges on markets and marketing. Recall that most unusual example already mentioned: John Fante's best book, *Ask the Dust* (1939), lost its advertising budget to bigger concerns that his publisher, Stackpole Sons, faced—a lawsuit by Adolf Hitler! Barolini's *Umbertina*, DeRosa's *Paper Fish*: these are great books, but when (with difficulty) they were first published they met with very limited success. The Feminist Press has republished these books, and the book catalogue for this press now has a section titled "Italian American." Once again, even as I write, women authors and critics are "claiming a tradition." "Through their work, these women," Giunta notes, "are sanctioning the literary existence of authors from a more distant past; in doing so, they are also validating their work as well as the work of other Italian American women in the future" (24).

Louisa Ermelino is one contemporary author who during recent years has staked a claim to this emerging tradition. To do so, she has, in her writing, accentuated boundaries and in transgressing them, her narrative has evolved from male-centered to female-centered fiction. In fact, across her three Spring Street novels, she has written men out of the narrative. Helen and Mary Mallone in Ermelino's third book of fiction first beat up sister Gracie's husband, Frankie Merrelli, and when that does not curtail his women chasing ways, they club him over the head and push him into the river; they eliminate Frankie so that sisterhood can prosper.

Ermelino's first novel takes place mostly on Spring Street, but frequently refers briefly to Las Vegas and ends there. *The Black Madonna* is set chiefly on Spring Street but moves briefly to the Bronx and, for a substantial section, to Castelfondo, Italy. *The Sisters Mallone* moves back and forth between Hell's Kitchen and the Spring Street neighborhood.

Joey Dee Gets Wise tells the story of a young Italian American man. *The Black Madonna* describes the relationships of three Italian American mothers and their sons. Ermelino's third novel narrates the adventures of three sisters and their grandmother. Characters in all three of these novels dream of escaping the confines of their neighborhood, temporarily move beyond its bounds or transcend the limitations of the block. All three novels explore the rewards and limitations of neighborhood: mapping it as sanctuary or trap. Who gets out of the neighborhood, by what means, and how far that character goes is interesting to note, another sort of American / Italian American negotiation. Whereas the male characters are all circumscribed in their perambulations, the sisters Mallone move freely beyond much that would fence them in.

Joey De Stefano is desperate to escape his neighborhood. He thinks constantly of starting anew in Las Vegas and daydreams about driving a Cadillac in the desert. In fact, this brief novel refers to Joey's fantasy twenty-one times. Yet as the novel progresses, Joey becomes more and more entrenched. Ironically, Joey does move to Las Vegas at the novel's conclusion, but not by his own initiative. The neighborhood strongman,

Nicky Mole (Malevento), sends him there; and when Joey arrives, he finds that he has never left Little Italy. Not only is he tied to Nicky and working for one of the casinos, but Mikey Bats, an old neighborhood pal, visits him there.

Nicky and Joey can be seen as two sides of the same coin. Joey surreptitiously dates Josie Magro, Carolina and Sonny's daughter; Nicky, in the same way, dates Carolina. Both men promise to wipe out the past for their women and—at least in their eyes—to free them by doing so (*Joey Dee* 112, 125). Nicky has Sonny pushed off a roof so that he can eventually marry Carolina. Joey, too, wants to be master of his own fate. The two men differ in that Joey cares what the neighborhood thinks, but Nicky does not; Joey sides with "the underdog" and Nicky "with the man of power" (143).

Carolina Magro is another character that seeks to control her own destiny. She shares with Joey not only allegiance to Nicky but also dread of the neighborhood regimen and restriction. "Joey Dee was afraid someone would see. He was always afraid of this. In the neighborhood someone would always see" (126). Carolina would not leave her apartment during the day because "'those hags on the park bench'" would "'throw their cheap curses'" (79-80). Because of her reputation and because of neighborhood mourning rituals, Carolina goes out only at night and only to meet Nicky Mole. This woman who would transgress or move past borders is kept locked in a room. She tells Joey, "'I hate this apartment [...] I'm here all day. It's like a goddamn dungeon'" (79).

Nicky, on the other hand, marries Carolina, adopts Josie, and moves "his new family to lower Fifth Avenue" (168). In other words, in Louisa Ermelino's first Spring Street novel the "man of power" is the one who most successfully transcends the limits of the ethnic neighborhood, but he does so by the most commonplace and narrow of preconceived Italian American ethnic means—as mobster.

Midway in Josephine Gattuso Hendin's 1988 novel *The Right Thing to Do* the protagonist, Gina Giardello, thinks, "there was a kind of redemption in escaping the place where you were born, the limits of the world around you" (198). For the characters in *Joey Dee Gets Wise* there is no redemption (not even for Nicky, who moves of his own will, but crimes as severe as murder make that move possible). Teresa Sabatini in *The Black Madonna* and Gracie (Mallone) Merrelli in *The Sisters Mallone* do experience redemption, but their redemption is not easy and they achieve it in spite of or against the neighborhood. So it is with Gina Giardello.

As Gina walks through her Astoria neighborhood one night with Alex, her Anglo boyfriend, the eyes of neighbors keep careful, if not intrusive, watch. Robert Orsi has noted that, "the life of the domus spilled out into closely watched streets and hallways. [...] Neighbors were expected to watch the behavior of each other's children [...] this insured that the standards and values of the domus would be maintained in the streets as well" (*Madonna of 115th Street* 92). Gina wants to escape the rigid rules that her father Nino insists that she follow. She wants an education and her independence. Yet, when she leaves Queens' Little Italy, she travels to Manhattan's Little Italy; when she rents a room farther uptown in Manhattan, it is hers and hers alone, not a room in her parent's apartment, and yet it is also drab, tight, and confining.

Manhattan holds promise for Gina, but Manhattan's promise is illusory: "the beauty of it receded before the familiar routine of drudge-work" (76). Gina attends college as well as doing her daily "drudge-work" job. At the start of the novel, family members discuss Gina's education. One relative says, "'Send a girl to school, you send her into trouble'" (22). Gina's mother Laura says, "What's wrong if she goes to college?" Although Laura defends her daughter, Laura sets precise boundaries: "'She could be an elementary school teacher. That's a good job for a woman'" (24). Gina, in the course of the novel, learns how to navigate and negotiate the worlds of Queens and Manhattan and the ways of Anglos and Italian Americans. She learns how to cross these boundaries at will, as if these restrictions were but low fences in her own backyard.

Like Gina Giardello, Teresa Sabatini in *The Black Madonna* learns to navigate neighborhoods and negotiate old and new ways. Unlike Gina, Teresa does so more for the sake of her son Nicky than for herself. All three sections of *The Black Madonna*—"Teresa: 1948," "Magdalena: 1936," and "Antoinette: 1968"—focus on the relationship between male and female characters but do not emphasize the character whose name the section bears. Indeed, Amadeo Pavese, for example, is at the center of the middle section. The focus of "Teresa: 1948" is the relationship between Teresa and her son, whom she is struggling to raise by herself in the absence of her husband, who—she believes—is at sea.

When Nicky is paralyzed by an accident that happens while he is playing with Antoinette's son Jumbo, she keeps him at home from school so that the neighbors will not see him so disabled. She takes him to doctors and to a local woman with claims to healing powers. For her son she negotiates old and new ways.

Eventually, Teresa learns that her husband is living in the Bronx with another wife. Teresa, who never leaves the neighborhood, travels to the Bronx, confronts the other wife, and visits her husband, who is ill in a hospital and soon dies. By defying the second wife and the wife's father, Teresa is able to return the body of her husband to the Spring Street neighborhood, thus, saving face and providing her son with his father—albeit dead. At the wake, Nicky regains his ability to walk.

Teresa, Magdalena, and Antoinette pray to the Black Madonna. Teresa keeps her Black Madonna hidden in her "top dresser drawer" (81) and Magdalena maintains a shrine to her in the attic of her house. Teresa's section of the novel ends with the sentence, "Always, there was the Black Madonna" (81). This Madonna, as Lucia Chiavola Birnbaum explains, is a secret one kept dear by women in a sisterhood of women. She notes: "Outwardly maintaining church forms, while silently retaining ancient beliefs, appears, in my research, to be the mode used by Italian peasants" (27), a mode often carried to America. According to Birnbaum, women hold on to this ancient Madonna because the institutional church "demoted" the Madonna "from goddess to saint" and reduced "her many characteristics [...] to obedience and patience [...]" (195). The Black Madonna represents women's claim to their own religious practice and power outside the bounds of the male-dominated church. In other words, the Black Madonna represents a transgression by Italian American women of male-authored rules, and *The Black Madonna* represents a transitional step in the movement of Ermelino's writing from male-centered narrative to a female-centered one.

Robert Orsi has articulated another conflict in the lives of Italian American women—between a private source of power and public display of humility: "Italian women lived under the pressure of two dangerously conflicting demands: that they exercise their power in the domus and that they appear powerless. Their exercise of power, therefore, was frequently clandestine" (147). So it is with Teresa, but not with the sisters Mallone. Yes, Mary and Helen act surreptitiously when they murder Frankie (murder is, after all, a crime), but in public they never act with humility and docility. In fact, at the funeral that opens *The Sisters Mallone*, the sisters are described as "outside the neighborhood [...] They drove cars. They smoked cigarettes" (15). They did not act like "proper" women.

Amadeo Pavese is the focus of "Magdalena: 1936," the second section of *The Black Madonna*. He travels far outside the neighborhood to the home village in Italy. However, his journey from Spring Street is not one of escape or liberation from the old neighborhood, but rather the means by which the neighborhood and the old ways attain a more secure grip on him. Amadeo knows that he has entered the old ways as he enters his aunt and uncle's house in Castelfondo. Zia Guinetta is the power behind the scenes in this section. Like Nicky Mole in *Joey Dee Gets Wise*, "Zia Guinetta believed in fate but she believed more in power" (113). In front of her Black Madonna she says, "'I am more clever than any man. [...] Why do my powers have to be dark and hidden?'" (113). In this way, she differs from Nicky Mole, whose power had to be visible to the neighborhood to be effective. His headquarters and his henchmen were in the open, on the street. Zia Guinetta uses her power to lead Amadeo into a marriage with Magdalena so that Salvatore, Amadeo's son whose mother died giving birth, will have a new mother and all will be set right with the prescribed rules of the world.

In "Antoinette: 1968," the third section of the novel, Nicky, Salvatore, and Jumbo are now men. All three are partially successful in leaving the neighborhood but remain very much tied to it. The old ways continue although thirty-two years have passed since Magdalena came to America as Amadeo's young bride. Marriage is one way by which the three men exit the neighborhood. Ironically, only Nicky, who has become a policeman, marries an Italian American, and their marriage fails. Sal has become a lawyer, and his *prominente* profession has taken him farther from the neighborhood. He lives in Connecticut with a blond-haired woman named Lindsey.

Most of the third section concerns Jumbo, Antoinette's son. Although he is the one most tied to home, mother, and neighborhood, he is also the one to go farthest a-field through marriage. Jumbo, an obese, debt-ridden bartender, has fallen in love with a Jewish schoolteacher from Long Island, Judy Bernstein. When their son is born Jumbo promises his mother to name the baby Salvatore and promises Judy's parents to name him Sol. This will work out fine: on Long Island the baby will be Sol, and on Spring Street he will be Sal, just a simple change of a single letter. This solution points to the fluidity of identity rather than to its rigidity.

But, some rigid rules remain. Jumbo has promised the Bernsteins that the baby would be raised Jewish; he has promised his mother that the baby would be baptized Catholic. The three friends plot a scheme for the baby's baptism. Nicky has arrested a man who impersonates a priest. It is simple: they will sneak into a church and have the man whom Nicky has arrested perform the baptism. Curiously, Salvatore is the one who gets cold feet. He "was uneasy, because Magdalena had always made him know that there was a greater power, an omnipotent one, and though he moved out in the world in custom pin-striped suits and slept with a golden blond woman [...], he knew there were lines you didn't

America / Trattabili • 173

cross [...]" (244-245). In other words, the one who has moved farthest away feels most constrained.

All goes well at the christening and afterward they have a party to which Magdalena comes, accompanied by Marilena, a young woman from Castelfondo. Marilena just appears here at the novel's close. Ermelino does not state how she got there or why. This is not a narrative error, but an appropriate element for the novel's end. It exemplifies once again women's magic or power and that the old ways—such as veneration of the male-outlawed Black Madonna—will continue and form the basis of a community of women, a source for women's strength outside the male domain. Ermelino writes, "Marilena didn't lower her eyes when Magdalena introduced her to Nicky. He noticed the strange amulet she wore at her throat on a black silk chord. He couldn't have known it was the polished black bone of a goat" (251-252). Nicky may have regained the ability to walk and have grown up to be a policeman, but borders remain that he cannot cross. One of those is entrance into the alternative world of an ancient female power.

In Ermelino's most recent novel, *The Sisters Mallone*, the sisters' power is their ability to cross many borders. The source of their fluidity, paradoxically, is their neighborhood. These Italian American sisters have grown up in an Irish neighborhood, Hell's Kitchen. Nonetheless, they remain Italian and move back and forth between the Irish neighborhood and the Italian one on Spring Street. This provides them with a freedom and perspective that other Ermelino characters do not enjoy. Carolina, for example, tells Joey near the end of the first Spring Street novel: "'Josie's different, like my mother, like me. We've always been different. Some people just don't get put where they belong'" (*Joey Dee* 166). The Mallone sisters, too, are different, but with the advantage that they are where they belong, which enables them to move from place to place and to express themselves fully. They are the mistresses of their own destinies.

There are, of course, males in *The Sisters Mallone*, but they are pawns of the sisters' or removed from the narrative by the forceful action of

Mary and Helen. Some of the males are reminiscent of characters in *Joey Dee Gets Wise*, Ermelino's first novel. This makes sense because half of the story of the later novel takes palce on Spring Street, and neighborhood has a strong shaping force in Ermelino's stories. Frankie Merelli, for example, is similar to Joey De Stefano. Ermelino says of the work that Joey's father finds for him, "For none of these jobs could he wear his Siegel Brothers shoes and sharkskin suits. They were all sweaty jobs, and Joey Dee hated to sweat" (26). These words could easily describe Frankie, who is also a pretty boy, does not like to sweat, and prefers to have occasion to wear Siegel Brothers shoes. Just as Joey keeps Josie on the side, Frankie keeps first Doreen and then Miranda; but the situations are different. Frankie is married and married to a Mallone sister. The sisters pledged to protect one another, a fact that gets Frankie in trouble and brings him to an early demise in the murk between pier and ship.

The Mallone sisters learn many lessons from their grandmother, Anona, which is in keeping with the female-centered community of the novel. Anona told her granddaughters about the time "right after she came over on the boat" that their grandfather "raised his hand to her" (54). When he fell asleep Anona, as she tells it, "'took the broom handle . . . Pow! Right on the head'" (54). The sisters love to hear this story. Although influenza carried off their mother, father, brother, and grandfather, Mary liked to speculate that Nona actually killed her husband and "Helen agreed, 'We're born man-killers,' she liked to say. 'We get it from the old lady'" (55).

The Sisters Mallon begins in the early 1950s and in short chapters, weaves back and forth in time. Although Frankie's funeral takes place in the second short chapter, it is not until near the end of the novel that the reader learns how Frankie died and who was responsible. Not until the end does the reader realize how well Mary and Helen learned Anona's lesson and how far they will go to protect little sister Gracie. At the conclusion, Gracie turns away from the protection of her older sisters and moves into an independent world of her own making and choosing.

Thus, she completes the powerful woman-based community just as DeSalvo turned away from her "older sister," Virginia Woolf, to be able to tell her own story.

After Frankie's death Gracie realizes, "they had fallen for each other [...] because both wanted more than was possible, more than was available to people like them. But they had slipped into the life everyone expected" (275). They had fallen into the trap and not a sanctuary or a paradise. After Frankie's death, Gracie has "a chance" to forge once more her own fate. "She wasn't the same woman who had come to this neighborhood as a bride," Ermelino explains. "She was terrified, and to tell the truth, strangely thrilled" (273).

Instead of calling on Helen and Mary, Gracie decides to figure things out for herself, including why Frankie had a strange key with him at the time of his death. She seeks the assistance of Vincent Violotti. True, he is a male lawyer, but the initiative is Gracie's; Violotti is her acquaintance, her connection. The key, they discover, unlocks a safety deposit box with "ten packets of bills" with "'$5G' written across" the top of each (287), money Frankie had hidden from his wife to be used for his trysts. Gracie receives money from Vito Genovese and also the union insurance. Helen and Mary's shove has set Gracie and her son Charlie up very nicely. But now Gracie, not her husband or her sisters, is in charge:

> I'm gonna move. Near the park. Fourth Street Park. I'm gonna look at the arch from my window. Yeah, I'm gonna move to Fourth Street Park and Charlie's gonna go to St. Joseph's Academy where all the money kids go. (288)

Earlier in the novel Gracie had walked to Forth Street. For the women, especially the wives, of Spring Street who were to stay on Spring Street, this walk, a transgression of community standards without the aid of her sisters, anticipates the end. "Gracie had stepped through the looking glass for one afternoon," Ermelino narrates. "Sitting there she couldn't believe how wide the world was, how she had locked herself into a box of a few city blocks" (129). A woman sitting next to Gracie on a park bench tells her she "'should consider moving'" to Fourth Street (129). Gracie thinks, "Why not? [...] Miracles happened every day" (129).

Whether it was a miracle that enabled her to move or the intervention of her sisters, this move is a woman-centered and woman-initiated one. Nicky Malevento moves his family, two women, to Fourth Street Park, but Nicky is a believer in men of power. In every way except destination, the move described at the end of Ermelino's most recent novel differs from the move described in her first one. Nicky kills Sonny, the father-husband, whereas Gracie does not know that her sisters killed her husband. Gracie had nothing to do with Frankie's death, but now that he is dead Gracie charts her own course for her new life.

Movement and expression are intertwined in Ermelino's fiction and that of other Italian Americans. To be stuck in neighborhood is to be stuck in attitude. To carry an old attitude to a new neighborhood is insufficient for true change. The old neighborhood is not necessarily a bad thing. Gina, in Hendin's novel, returns for her father's funeral and comes to appreciate the old ways even if she will predominantly lead her life in the new ways. The novel's author, Josephine Gattuso Hendin, says that she had to get out of her neighborhood, yet "after being away from my background for a great many years I discovered how connected I was to it and how much I had derived from it. In many ways the book [*The Right Thing to Do*] is a kind of love letter to that [...]" ("*VIA* Interview" 53). Marianna De Marco Torgovnick in her memoir-essay "On Being White, Female, and Born in Bensonhurst," notes her success in the world far beyond the neighborhood but also states, "You can take the girl out of Bensonhurst (that much is clear); but you may not be able to take Benshonhurst out of the girl" (10). According to De Marco Torgovnick, "Bensonhurst is a neighborhood dedicated to believing that its values are the only values; it tends towards certain forms of inertia" (7). In this rigid neighborhood, she adds, "Difference is not only unwelcome it is unacceptable" (7-8). Differences, however, are a necessity for a full life in the wide world. She remains Italian American but "a lot of other things as well" (16). Mary, Helen, and Gracie know about fluid identity and use this knowledge to their advantage whether in Hell's Kitchen or Little Italy. Expressing themselves encourages them to transcend boundaries and free movement encourages them to express themselves. The Italian American women's literary corpus transforms old strictures into new songs of beauty and praise as well as rebellion and change. May we all go forth and sing.

WORKS CITED

Albanese, Catherine L. "Introduction." *A Cobbler's Universe: Religion, Poetry, and Performance in the Life of a South Italian Immigrant.* Frank S. Spiziri. NY: Continuum, 1997. 21-102;

Auster, Paul. "The Art of Hunger." *The Art of Hunger: Essays, Prefaces, Interviews.* LA: Sun & Moon P, 1992. 9-20;

_____. *Hand to Mouth: A Chronicle of Early Failure.* NY: Holt, 1997;

Barbarese, J. T. *The Black Beach.* Denton, TX: U of North Texas P, 2005;

_____. "Danielle." *Margie: The American Journal of Poetry.* www.margiereview.com;

_____. Email Correspondence. 4 April—8 June 2004;

_____. "Featured Poet, J. T. Barbarese." *Italian Americana* 21.2 (2003): 187-188;

_____. "Inside Bradlee's Department Store." Unpublished poem;

_____. "Lessons in Race, Stereotyping: Is It Just a State of Mind?" *The Philadelphia Inquirer* February 4, 2003: B2;

_____. *New Science.* Athens, GA: U of Georgia P, 1989;

_____. *Under the Blue Moon.* Athens, GA: U of Georgia P, 1985;

_____. *A Very Small World.* Alexandria, VA: Orchises P, 2004;

Barker, Reginald, dir. *The Italian.* Paramount, 1915;

Barolini, Helen. "Buried Alive by Language." *Chiaroscuro: Essays of Identity.* Madison: U of Wisconsin P, 1999. 64-69;

_____. "A Calabrian Journey and Return." *Italian Americana* 20.1 (2002): 75-81;

_____. "Introduction." *The Dream Book.* 1985. Ed. Helen Barolini. Syracuse: Syracuse UP, 2000. 3-55;

_____. "The Nordic Type." *More Italian Hours and Other Stories.* Boca Raton, FL: Bordighera, 2001. 49-59;

_____. *Their Other Side: Six American Women and the Lure of Italy.* NY: Fordham UP, 2006;

_____. *Umbertina.* 1979. NY: Feminist Press, 1999;

Barone, Dennis, ed. *Beyond the Red Notebook: Essays on Paul Auster*. Phila. U of Pennsyvania P, 1995;

_____. "Cairns." *Wild Dreams: The Best of Italian Americana*. Carol Bonomo Albright and Joanna Clapps Herman, eds. NY: Fordham UP, 2008. 275-282;

_____. "An Interview with Gilbert Sorrentino." *Partisan Review* 48 (1981): 236-246;

_____. "An Introduction to William Smith and Rhetoric at the College of Philadelphia." *Proceedings of the American Philosophical Society* 134.2 (1990): 111-160;

_____. "A 'Natural' Environment: Hollywood." *American Studies* 36.2 (1995): 83-97;

_____, ed. Paul Auster half-issue. *Review of Contemporary Fiction* 14.1 (1994): 7-96;

_____, ed. Toby Olson half-issue. *Review of Contemporary Fiction* 11.2 (1991): 114-224;

_____. *Walking Backwards*. Florence, MA: Quale Press, 2002;

Barone, Dennis and Peter Ganick, eds. *The Art of Practice: Forty-Five Contemporary Poets*. Elmwood, CT: Potes & Poets P, 1994;

Baudrillard, Jean. *America*. London: Verso, 1988;

Benet, William Rose. Rev. of *Son of Italy*, by Pascal D'Angelo. *Saturday Review of Literature* 27 December, 1924: 411;

_____. "Round about Parnassus." *Saturday Review of Literature* 26 March, 1932: 620;

Bertellini, Giorgio. "Italian Imageries, Historical Feature Films, and the Fabrication of Italy's Spectators in Early 1900s New York." *American Movie Audiences: From the Turn of the Century to the Early Sound Era*. Melvin Stokes and Richard Maltby, eds. London: BFI, 1999. 29-45;

_____. "New York City and the Representation of Italian Americans in the Cinema." *The Italians of New York: Five Centuries of Struggle and Achievement*. Philip V. Cannistraro, ed. NY: The New-York Historical Society and The John D. Calandra Italian American Institute, 2000. 115-128;

Biale, David. "The Melting Pot and Beyond: Jews and the Politics of American Identity." *Insider/Outsider: American Jews and Multiculturalism*. David Biale, Michael Galchinsky, and Susan Herschel, eds. Berkeley: U of CA P, 1998. 17-33;

Birnbaum, Lucia Chiavola. *Black Madonnas: Feminism, Religion, and Politics in Italy*. Boston: Northeastern UP, 1993;

Bodei, Remo. *We, the Divided: Ethos, Politics and Culture in Post-War Italy, 1943-2006*. NY: Agincourt, 2006;

Boelhower, William. "The Right Promethean Fire." *Immigrant Autobiography in the United States: Four Versions of the Italian American Self*. Verona: Essedue edizioni, 1982. 97-135;

Bok, Edward. *The Americanization of Edward Bok*. NY: Scribners, 1920;

Bona, Mary Jo. *Claiming a Tradition: Italian American Women Writers*. Carbondale: Southern Illinois UP, 1999;

Bondanella, Peter. *Hollywood Italians: Dagos, Palokas, Romeos, Wise Guys, and Sopranos*. NY: Continuum, 2004;

Brodhead, Richard. "Strangers on a Train: The Double Dream of Italy in the American Gilded Age." *Modernism/Modernity* 1.2 (1994): 1-19;

Bruegmann, Robert. *Sprawl: A Compact History*. Chicago: U of Chicago P, 2005;

Bryant, Dorothy. *Miss Giardino*. 1978. NY: The Feminist P, 1997;

Cain, James M. "Camera Obscura." *The American Mercury* (Oct. 1933): 138-146;

Calvino, Italo. *Marcovaldo or The seasons in the City*. 1963. San Diego: Harcourt Brace, 1983;

Carnevali, Emanuel. *Furnished Rooms*. Edited and with an Afterword by Dennis Barone. NY: Bordighera Press, 2006;

Castellblanch, Ramon. "Latinos' Opinions as Varied as Their Backgrounds." *The Hartford Courant* 8 August 2003: A11;

Collins, Richard. *John Fante: A Literary Portrait*. Toronto: Guernica Editions, 2000;

Conzen, Kathleen, David Gerber, Ewa Morawska, George E. Pozzetta, and Rudolph J. Vecoli. "The Invention of Ethnicity: A Perspective from the U.S.A." *Journal of American Ethnic History* 12.1 (1992): 3-41;

Cooper, Stephen. *Full of Life: A Biography of John Fante*. NY: North Point P, 2000;

Corsi, Edward. *In the Shadow of Liberty: The Chronicle of Ellis Island*. NY: Macmillan, 1935;

D'Alfonso, Antonio. Email Correspondence. 24 September 2003;

D'Angelo, Pascal. *Son of Italy*. NY: Macmillan, 1924;

_____. "The Toilers." *The Literary Digest* 14 October 1922: 42;

Daniell, Tina. "Philip Dunne: Fine Cabinetmaker." *Backstory: Interviews with Screenwriters of Hollywood's Golden Age*. Pat McGilligan, ed. Berkeley: U of California P, 1986. 151-169;

De Marco Torgovnic, Marianna. *Crossing Ocean Parkway*. Chicago: U of Chicago P, 1996;

De Rosa, Tina. *Paper Fish*. 1980. NY: The Feminist P, 1996;

DeSalvo, Louise. *Adultery*. Boston: Beacon P, 1999;

_____. *Crazy in the Kitchen: Food, Feuds, and Forgiveness in an Italian American Family*. NY: Bloomsbury, 2004;

_____. *Vertigo: A Memoir*. NY: Penguin, 1996;

DeSalvo, Louise and Edvige Giunta. "Introduction." *The Milk of Almonds: Italian American Women Writers on Food and Culture*. Louise DeSalvo and Edvige Giunta, eds. NY: The Feminist P, 2002. 1-13;

Di Donato, Pietro. *Christ in Concrete*. 1939. New York: Penguin, 1993;

_____. *Three Circles of Light*. New York: Julian Messner, 1960;

Dmytryk, Edward, dir. *Give Us This Day*. J. Arthur Rank, 1949 (film version of *Christ in Concrete*);

Domini, John. *Earthquake I.D.* Los Angeles: Red Hen P, 2007;

Dubord, Guy. *Comments on the Society of the Spectacle*. London: Verso, 1990;

_____. *The Society of the Spectacle*. NY: Zone Books, 1994;

Dunne, John Gregory. *Monster: Living Off the Big Screen*. NY: Random House, 1997;

Emerson, Ralph Waldo. "Gifts." *Essays: First and Second Series Complete in One Volume*. NY: Thomas Y. Crowell, 1951: 374-379;

_____. "History" and "Self-Reliance." *Selected Essays*. Larzar Ziff, ed. NY: Penguin Books: 1982: 149-173 and 175-203;

Equi, Elaine. Email Correspondence. 14 September 2003;

_____. "What Is American About American Poetry?" 6 Feb. 2002 http://www. poetrysociety.org/equi;

Ermelino, Louisa. *The Black Madonna*. NY: Simon & Schuster, 2001;

_____. *Joey Dee Gets Wise*. NY: St. Martin's P, 1991;

_____. *The Sisters Mallone*. NY: Simon & Schuster, 2002;

Fante, John. *Ask the Dust*. 1939. Santa Rosa, CA: Black Sparrow P, 1980;

_____. *The Brotherhood of the Grape*. 1977. Santa Rosa, CA: Black Sparrow P, 1988;

_____. "John Fante's Diary." *Selected Letters: 1932-1981*. Seamus Cooney, ed. Santa Rosa, CA: Black Sparrow P, 1991. 315-324;

_____. *Dreams from Bunker Hill*. Santa Rosa, CA: Black Sparrow P, 1982;

_____. *Fante / Mencken: John Fante & H. L. Mencken: A Personal Correspondence: 1930-1952*. Michael Moreau, ed. Santa Rosa, CA: Black Sparrow P, 1989;

_____. *Full of Life*. 1952. Santa Rosa, CA: Black Sparrow P, 1988;

_____. *The John Fante Reader*. Stephen Cooper, ed. NY: William Morrow, 2002;

_____. *My Dog Stupid*. *West of Rome*. Santa Rosa, CA: Black Sparrow P, 1986. 9-143;

_____. *1933 Was a Bad Year*. Santa Rosa, CA: Black Sparrow P, 1985;

_____. "The Odyssey of a Wop." *The Wine of Youth: Selected Stories*. Santa Rosa: Black Sparrow P, 1985. 133-146;

_____. *The Road to Los Angeles*. (Written 1933-1936.) Santa Rosa, CA: Black Sparrow P, 1999.

_____. *Selected Letters: 1932 to 1981*. Seamus Conney, ed. Santa Rosa, CA: Black Sparrow P, 1991;

_____. *Wait Until Spring, Bandini*. 1938. Santa Rosa, CA: Black Sparrow P, 1983;

Faulkner, William. "Golden Land." *Collected Stories of William Faulkner*. NY: Random House, 1950. 701-726;

Federal Writers' Project, Works Progress Administration in the City of New York. *The Italians of New York*. New York: Random House, 1938;

Fine, Richard. *Hollywood and the Profession of Authorship, 1928-1940*. Ann Arbor: U of Michigan P, 1985;

Fitzgerald, F. Scott. *The Last Tycoon*. 1941. NY: Collier Books, 1986;

Forgione, Louis. *Men of Silence*. NY: Dutton, 1928;

_____. *Reamer Lou*. NY: Dutton, 1924;

_____. *The River Between*. NY: Dutton, 1928;

Forman, Henry James. *Our Movie Made Children*. NY: Macmillan, 1933;

Freund, David M. P. "Marketing the Free Market: State Intervention and the Politics of Prosperity in Metropolitan American." *The New Suburban History*. Kevin M. Kruse and Thomas J. Sugrue, eds. Chicago: Chicago UP, 2006.11-32;

Friedman, Lester D. "Celluloid Palimpsests: An Overview of Ethnicity and the American Film." *Unspeakable Images: Ethnicity and the American Cinema*. Lester D. Friedman, ed. Urbana: U of Illinois P, 1991. 11-35;

Gambino, Richard. *Blood of My Blood*. 1974. Toronto: Guernica Editions, 2000;

_____. "The Crisis of Italian American identity." *Beyond the Godfather: Italian American Writers on the Real Italian American Experience*. A. Kenneth Ciongoli and Jay Parini, eds. Hanover, NH: UP of New England, 1997. 269-288;

Gans, Herbert J. "Symbolic Ethnicity: The Future of Ethnic Groups and Cultures in America." *On the Making of Americans: Essay in Honor of David Riesman*. Herbert J. Gans, Nathan Glazer, Joseph R. Gusfeld, and Christopher Jencks, eds. Philadelphia: U of Pennsylvania P, 1979. 193-220;

Gardaphé, Fred L. *Italian Signs, American Streets: The Evolution of Italian American Narrative*. Durham: Duke UP, 1996;

_____. *Leaving Little Italy: Essaying Italian American Culture*. Albany: SUNY P, 2004;

Gillan, Maria Mazziotti. "Public School 18: Paterson, New Jersey." *The Dream Book*. Helen Barolini, ed. Syracuse: Syracuse UP, 2000: 320-321;

Gioia, Dana. "Strong Counsel." *Can Poetry Matter? Essays On Poetry and American Culture*. Saint Paul, MN: Graywolf P, 1991. 47-60;

_____. "What Is Italian American Poetry?" *Beyond The Godfather: Italian American Writers on the Real Italian American Experience*. A Kenneth Ciongoli and Jay Parini, eds. Hanover, NH: UP of New England, 1997. 167-174;

Giunta, Edvige. *Writing with an Accent: Contemporary Italian American Women Authors*. NY: Palgrave, 2002;

Giunta, Edvige and Kathleen Zamboni McCormick, eds. *Teaching Italian American Literature, Film, and Popular Culture*. NY: MLA, 2010;

Gordon, Neil. "Shanghaied in Tinseltown." *Salon.com*. May 12, 2000;

Gordon, Richard E.; Gordon, Katherine K.; and Gunther, Max. *The Split-Level Trap*. 1960. NY: Dell, 1964;

Grant, Madison. *The Passing of the Great Race or The Racial Bias of European History*. NY: Scribner's Sons, 1916;

Green, Alfred E., dir. *East of the River*. Screen Play by Fred Niblo, Jr. From the Original Story by John Fante and Ross B. Wills. Warner Bros., 1940;

Hallowell, A. Irving. "The Self in Its Behavioral Environment." *Culture and Experience*. 1955. New York: Schocken Books, 1967. 75-110;

Hendin, Josephine Gattuso. *The Right Thing to Do*. 1988. NY: The Feminist P, 1999;

Isherwood, Christopher. *A Single Man*. 1964. NY: Farrar, Straus and Giroux, 1993;

Jacobson, Matthew Frye. *Whiteness of a Different Color: European Immigrants and the Alchemy of Race*. Cambridge: Harvard UP, 1998;

James, Henry. *Daisy Miller: A Study*. 1878. NY: Penguin Books, 1988;

Juliani, Richard N. *Building Little Italy: Philadelphia Italians Before Mass Migration*. University Park, PA: Penn State UP, 1998;

_____. "Community and Identity: Continuity and Change Among Italian Americans in Philadelphia." *The Italian American Review* 6.2 (1997-1998): 42-59;

Jurca, Catherine. *White Diaspora: The Suburb and the Twentieth-Century American Novel*. Princeton: Princeton UP, 2001;

Kallen, Horace M. *Culture and Democracy in the United States*. NY: Boni and Liveright, 1924;

Kellor, Frances A. "What Is Americanization?" *Yale Review* 8 (1919): 282-299;

Kordich, Catherine J. *John Fante: His Novels and Novellas*. NY: Twayne Publishers, 2000;

Krieger, Alex. "The Costs—and Benefits?—of Sprawl." *Sprawl and Suburbia*. William S. Saunders, ed. Minneapolis: U of Minnesota P, 2005. 44-56;

Kuhn, Thomas S. *The Structure of Scientific Revolutions*. Second Edition. Chicago: U of Chicago P, 1970;

Lankevich, George J. *American Metropolis: A History of New York City*. New York: New York UP, 1998;

Lape, Esther Everett. "Putting America into Your City." *The Ladies' Home Journal* Sept. 1919: 35-37;

Lapolla, Garibaldi M. "These, Parents, Are Our Schools." Balch Manuscript, Group 64, Box 1, Folder 12. Historical Society of Pennsylvania. Philadelphia, Pennsylvania;

Laurino, Maria. *Were You Always an Italian? Ancestors and Other Icons of Italian America.* NY: Norton, 2000;

Lawton, Ben. "Mafia and the Movies: Why is Italian American Synonymous with Organized Crime?" *Screening Ethnicity: Cinematographic Representations of Italian Americans in the United States.* Anna Camaiti Hostert and Anthony Julian Tamburri, eds. Boca Raton: Bordighera P, 2002. 69-95;

Leopardi, Giacomo. *The Canti with a selection of his prose.* J. G. Nichols, trans. Manchester: Carcanet, 1998;

Levi, Carlo. *Christ Stopped at Eboli: The Story of a Year.* 1945. NY: Farrar, Straus and Giroux, 2006;

Lindsay, Vachel. *The Art of the Motion Picture.* 1915. NY: Liveright, 1970;

"Louis Forgione." *The Bookman* March-August, 1925: 126-127;

Luconi, Stefano. "The Protean Ethnic Identities of John Fante's Italian-American Characters." *John Fante: A Critical Gathering.* Stepen Cooper and David Fine, eds. Madison, NJ: Fairleigh Dickinson UP, 1999. 54-64;

MacLeod, Christian (Anna Ruddy). *The Heart of the Stranger: A Story of Little Italy.* NY: Fleming H. Revell Company, 1908;

Mangano, Antonio. "The Effect of Emigration upon Italy." 1908. *The Ordeal of Assimilation: A Documentary History of the White Working Class, 1830s to the 1970s.* Stanley Feldstein and Lawrence Costello, eds. Garden City, NY: Anchor Books, 1974. 17-24;

Mangione, Jerre. "A Double Life: The Fate of the Urban Ethnic." *Literature and the Urban Experience: Essays on the City and Literature.* Michael C. Jaye and Ann Chalmers Watts, eds. New Brunswick: Rutgers UP, 1981. 169-183;

_____. "Finale." *Mount Allegro: A Memoir of Italian American Life.* Syracuse: Syracuse UP, 1998. 287-309;

_____. "Italian-American Novelists." *New Republic* 104 (January 6, 1941): 20;

_____. *Mount Allegro: A Memoir of Italian American Life.* 1942. Syracuse: Syracuse UP, 1998;

Mann, D. L. Rev. of *Son of Italy*, by Pascal D'Angelo. *Boston Transcript* 6 December 1924: 5;

Mannino, Mary Ann. "In Our Ears, A Voice: The Persistence of the Trauma of Immigration in *Blue Italian* and *Umbertina*." *Italian Americana* 20.1 (2002): 5-13;

Mariano, John Horace. *The Italian Contribution to American Democracy.* Boston: Christopher Publishing, 1921;

Marshall, Alex. *How Cities Work: Suburbs, Sprawl, and The Roads Not Taken.* Austin: U of Texas P, 2000;

Montemarano, Nicholas. *A Fine Place.* NY: Context Books, 2002;

Murphy, Jim. *Pick & Shovel Poet: The Journeys of Pascal D'Angelo.* NY: Clarion Books, 2002;

Nietzsche, Friedrich. *Thus Spoke Zarathustra. The Portable Nietzsche.* Walter Kaufmann, trans. and ed. NY: Viking, 1954. 103-439;

"Obituary. Joe [Jo] Pagano." *Variety* 306 (April 14, 1982): 98;

Olcott, Sidney, dir. *Poor Little Peppina.* Famous Players Film Company, 1916;

Orsi, Robert Anthony. "The Fault of Memory: 'Southern Italy' in the Imagination of Immigrants and the Lives of Their Children in Italian Harlem, 1920-1945." *Journal of Family History* 15.2 (1990): 133-147;

_____. *The Madonna of 115th Street: Faith and Community in Italian Harlem, 1880-1950.* New Haven: Yale UP, 1985;

Pagano, Jo. *The Condemned.* 1947. NY: Doubleday, 1954;

_____. "The Disinherited." *Editor's Choice.* Alfred Dashiell, ed. NY: G. P. Putnam's Sons, 1934. 312-326;

_____. *Golden Wedding.* NY: Random House, 1943;

_____. *The Paesanos.* Boston: Little, Brown and Co., 1940;

Panunzio, Constantine. *Immigration Crossroads.* NY: Macmillan, 1927;

_____. "Particles of Dust." *The Saturday Review of Literature* 1 (May 2, 1925): 723;

Papaleo, Joseph. "Arete." *The Dial* 2 (1960): 3-61;

_____. "Browlined 2049 AD Crystal Ball: Life A Peppery Allegory." *The Campus*, April 20, 1949: 2&3. Sarah Lawrence College Archives. Bronxville, NY;

_____. "History Lesson For Friday." *Picasso at 91.* Harriman, NY: Seaport Poets & Writers P, 1987. 30;

_____. *Italian Stories.* Normal, IL: Dalkey Archive P, 2002;

_____. "Joe Papaleo Discovers Particle Of Hope For A Radio-Cinematic Brave New World." *The Campus*, April 13, 1949: 3. Sarah Lawrence College Archives. Bronxville, NY;

_____. *Out of Place*. Boston: Little, Brown, 1970;

_____. "The Tony Chapter." Manuscript. Sarah Lawrence College Archives. Bronxville, NY;

Parati, Graziella. *Migration Italy: The Art of Talking Back in a Destination Culture*. Toronto: U of Toronto P, 2005;

Pavese, Cesare. *The Moon and the Bonfires*. 1950. NY: New York Review Books, 2002;

Peragallo, Olga. "Louis Forgione." *Italian-American Authors and Their Contributions to American Literature*. Anita Peragallo, ed. NY: S. F. Vanni, 1949. 105-108;

"Perfect Weekend 1990." *Sarah Lawrence Magazine*, Fall/Winter 1990-1991: 8-9. Sarah Lawrence College Archives. Bronxville, NY;

Pleasants, Ben. "The Last Interview of John Fante." *Los Angeles Times Magazine* 39.2 (February 1994): 90-95;

"Poet from the Slums." *Literary Digest* 8 April 1922. 34-35;

Puzo, Mario. *The Fortunate Pilgrim*. 1964. New York: Ballantine, 1998;

Quinn, Roseanne Giannini. "'We were working on an erotic song cycle': Reading Carole Maso's *AVA* as Poetics of Female Italian-American Cultural and Sexual Identity." *MELUS* 26.1 (2001): 91-113;

Radhakrishnan. R. "Is the Ethnic 'Authentic' in the Diaspora?" *Diasporic Mediations: Between Home and Location*. Minneapolis: U of Minnesota P, 1996: 203-214;

Report of the Committee on Americanization. Brooklyn: Italian Baptist Missionary Association, 1918;

Rev. of *Son of Italy*, by Pascal D'Angelo. *New York Times Book Review* 4 January 1925: 18;

Riis, Jacob A. *How The Other Half Lives*. 1890. NY: Penguin Books, 1997;

_____. *The Making of an American*. NY: Macmillan, 1901;

Rolle, Andrew. *The Italian Americans: Troubled Roots*. 1980. Norman, OK: U of Oklahoma P, 1984;

Rosenfeld, Isaac. "The Situation of the Jewish Writer." 1944. *Preserving the Hunger: An Isaac Rosenfeld Reader.* Mark Shechner, ed. Detroit: Wayne State UP, 1988. 121-123;

Ruotolo, Lucio. "Onorio Ruotolo and the Leonardo da Vinci Art School." *The Italian American Review* 7.2 (2000): 1-20;

Saroyan, William. *The Time of Your Life: A Comedy in Three Acts.* 1939. NY: Samuel French, 1941;

Sklar, Robert. *City Boys: Cagney, Bogart, Garfield.* Princeton: Princeton UP, 1992;

Speranza, Gino. "Does Americanization Americanize?" *The Atlantic Monthly* (Feb. 1920): 263-269;

_____. *Race or Nation: A Conflict of Divided Loyalties.* 1923. Indianapolis: Bobbs-Merrill, 1925;

Spiziri, Frank S. *A Cobbler's Universe: Religion, Poetry, and Performance in the Life of a South Italian Immigrant.* Edited and Translated, with an Introduction and Notes by Catherine L. Albanese. NY: Continuum, 1997;

Spotnitz, Frank. "The Hottest Dead Man in Hollywood." *American Film* 14.9 (1989): 40-44, 54;

Steinberg, Stephen. *The Ethnic Myth: Race, Ethnicity and Class in America.* New York: Atheneum, 1981;

Szliard, Leo. "Report on 'Grand Central Terminal'." *The Voice of the Dolphins and Other Stories.* New York: Simon and Schuster, 1961. 115-122;

Talese, Gay. "Where Are the Italian American Novelists?" *The New York Times Book Review* 14 March 1993: 1, 23, 25, 29;

Tamburri, Anthony Julian. *To Hyphenate or Not to Hyphenate.* Montreal: Guernica, 1991;

Tichi, Cecelia. *Shifting Gears: Technology, Literature, Culture in Modernist America.* Chapel Hill: U of North Carolina P, 1987;

Trachtenberg, Alan. *The Incorporation of America: Culture and Society in the Gilded Age.* New York: Hill & Wang, 1982;

"Triumph of Pascal D'Angelo: Pick and shovel Poet." *Literary Digest* 7 March 1925: 44-50;

Van Doren, Carl. "Introduction." Pascal D'Angelo, *Son of Italy.* NY: Macmillan, 1924. ix-xiii;

_____. "Journalism," Part One. *Three Worlds.* NY: Harper, 1936. 128-134;

———. "Through Ellis Island." *The Roving Critic*. NY: Knopf, 1923. 238-243;

Vecoli, Rudolph J. "Are Italian Americans Just White Folks?" *Beyond the Godfather: Italian American Writers on the Real Italian American Experience*. A. Kenneth Ciongoli and Jay Parini, eds. Hanover, NH: UP of New England, 1997. 307-318;

Venturi, Robert. *Complexity and Contradiction in Architecture*. Second Edition. NY: Museum of Modern Art, 1977;

———. "Sweet and Sour." *Architecture* 83.5 (May 1994): 51-52;

Venturi, Robert; Scott Brown, Denise; and Izenour, Steven. *Learning From Las Vegas*. Revised Edition. Cambridge: The MIT P, 1977;

"VIA Interviews Josephine Gattuso Hendin." *Voices in Italian Americana* 1.1 (1990): 53-62;

Welles, Orson, dir. *Citizen Kane*. RKO, 1941;

Wills, Ross B. "John Fante." 1941. *John Fante. Selected Letters, 1932-1981*. Seamus Cooney, ed. Santa Rosa, CA: Black Sparrow P, 1991. 329-338;

Wilson, Sloan. *The Man in the Grey Flannel Suit*. 1955. London: Remploy, 1972;

Wise, Gene. "'Paradigm Dramas' in American Studies: A Cultural and Institutional History of the Movement." *American Quarterly* 31 (1979): 293-337;

Woods, Katherine. Review of *The Paesanos*. *New York Times Book Review*. July 14, 1940: 7.

Yans-McLaughlin, Virginia. "Metaphors of Self in History: Subjectivity, Oral Narrative, and Immigration Studies." *Immigration Reconsidered: History, Sociology, and Politics*. Virginia Yans-McLaughlin, ed. New York: Oxford UP, 1990. 254-290.

Index

Adultery (DeSalvo), 90
"Ah, Poor America" (Fante), 99
Albanese, Catherine, 154–155
Alexius, 50
Amalfi, Italy, 147–149
Americanization
    anger of immigrants and, 67–69, 77–86
    belonging and, 101–102
    "big box" stores and, 152–154, 157–162
    comparisons of, 38–39
    defined, 12, 47
    ethnicity and, 21–23, 72–77
    lack of, in film depictions, 30–32, 36–37
    religion and, 1, 41–42
    stereotypes and, 143–144
American Studies movement, 11–18
Anger of immigrants, 67–69, 77–86
"Arete" (Papaleo), 140–141
The Art of Practice (Barone and Ganick), 6
Ask the Dust (Fante), 101, 118
Assimilation. *See* Americanization
Auster, Paul, 63–64
Authors, major compared to minor, 3–4
    See also specific authors
Automobile culture, 142–143, 145–148

Barbarese, J. T., 152, 154, 156–162
Barolini, Helen
    The Dream Book, 68, 77, 165
    on Italian American women writers, 166–167
    Their Other Side, 138, 139–140
    "The Nordic Type," 93–94

Umbertina, 70, 71, 92–93, 137–138, 156
Barone, Alfred, 2, 8
Barone, Alfredo, 1–3, 43
Barone, Dennis, 3–6
Barone, Melchisedec, 2
BASCO stores, 158
Baudrillard, Jean, 150
Beban, George, 28, 31–32
Belonging and Americanization, 101–102
Benet, William Rose, 61
Bensonhurst, 177
Bertellini, Giorgio, 29–30, 32
Biale, David, 92
"Big box" stores and assimilation, 152–154, 157–162
The Black Madonna (Ermelino), 164–165, 168, 171–174
Boaz, Franz, 10
Bodei, Remo, 142
Boelhower, William, 38n1, 56
Bok, Edward, 38–42, 45–46
Bona, Mary Jo, 165, 167
Bondanella, Peter, 31
Brodhead, Richard H., 29
The Brotherhood of the Grape (Fante), 119
Brown, Denise Scott, 158
Bruegmann, Robert, 141–142
Bryant, Dorothy Calvetti, 67–69, 77–78, 85

Cain, James M., 109–110, 120
California depiction, 129–130, 133–134, 145–146
Calvino, Italo, 140
Castellblanch, Ramon, 18
Christ in Concrete (di Donato), 25–26, 48, 55, 58, 76, 76n6, 79

Claiming a Tradition (Bona), 165
Collins, Richard, 107
Commissary system, 57
Complexity and Contradiction in Architecture (Venturi), 157–159
The Condemned (Pagano), 122, 123, 126–127
Conformity, 136–137
Consumerism, 138, 139–140, 142, 147–148
Conzen, Kathleen, 21–22
Cooney, Seamus, 114
Cooper, Stephen, 87, 95, 106–108, 114, 120
Corruption, corporate, 79–80
Corruption of sources, 16
Corsi, Edward, 68–69, 74, 76
Crazy in the Kitchen (DeSalvo), 139
Crime depictions, 29–30
Crossing Ocean Parkway (De Marco Torgovnick), 48
Cultural Studies movement, 18
Culture and Democracy in the United States (Kallen), 37
Culture and experience, 14–17

D'Angelo, Pascal
  chronology of life, 51–53, 64–66
  "Light," 63
  as marginalized from the margin, 48–49
  as migratory immigrant, 46–47
  as minor literary celebrity, 51
  publication of poems, 50–51, 52
  "The Toilers," 40–41, 75–76
  views on language/literacy, 59–62
  See also Son of Italy (D'Angelo)
"Danielle" (Barbarese), 159
Debord, Guy, 152
De Marco Torgovnick, Marianna, 48, 177–178

De Rosa, Tina, 89–90
DeSalvo, Louise
  Adultery, 90
  Crazy in the Kitchen, 139
  The Milk of Almonds, 166, 167
  Vertigo, 163–164, 166
  on Virginia Woolf, 166
Destiny, 23–24
Detroit Walls, 136n1
The Dial (Papaleo), 140–141
Di Donato, Pietro, 25–26, 48, 55, 58, 76, 76n6, 79
"The Disinherited" (Pagano), 122–123
Diversity of immigrants, 18–23
The Dream Book (Barolini), 68, 165
Dreams from Bunker Hill (Fante), 101–102, 115–116
Dunne, John Gregory, 109
Dunne, Philip, 110

East Coast connections, 110–111
East of the River (Fante), 97, 97n3
Education, 59–61, 166
  See also Literacy
Emerson, Ralph Waldo, 15, 25, 27, 91, 91n1, 138, 155, 157
Equi, Elaine, 163–164, 166
Ermelino, Louisa
  The Black Madonna, 164–165, 168, 171–174
  Joey Dee Gets Wise, 164–165, 168–170, 172, 175
  The Sisters Mallone, 164–165, 168, 172, 174–178
Escape/sanctuary
  America as, 82–83
  Italy as, 87–90, 98–99, 102–103, 104–105, 137–138
Ethnicity, 21–23, 72–77
Ethnographic approach to American Studies, 13, 17–18

Family, 58–59, 104
Fante, John
    "Ah, Poor America," 99
    Ask the Dust, 101, 118
    aspirations, 97–98
    The Brotherhood of the Grape, 119
    changing depictions of Italy, 87–88
    distracting habits, 119–121
    Dreams from Bunker Hill, 101–102, 115–116
    East of the River, 97, 97n3
    Full of Life, 100–101, 119
    Italian experiences, 95–96
    as model for "marble-game [pinball] maniac," 106
    movies depicted in works, 111–113
    My Dog Stupid, 87, 102–104, 117–118, 124
    1933 Was a Bad Year, 100, 111–112
    "The Odyssey of a Wop," 73
    Pagano comparison, 122–124
    The Road to Los Angeles, 63, 101, 112
    screenwriting of, 107–111, 113–115, 117–120
    Wait Until Spring, Bandini, 87, 97, 98–99, 112–113
Fascism, 127–129
"The Fault of Memory" (Orsi), 87–88, 104
Federal Writers' Project, 19
Fenton, Frank, 115
Films/film industry
    Hollywood and the Profession of Authorship, 1928-1940, 109
    Hollywood Italian, 31
    impact on youth, 36–37
    The Italian, 28–29, 31–34, 37
    Poor Little Peppina, 28–29, 31–32, 34–36, 37
    screenwriting and literary writing, 107–111
Fine, Richard, 109, 110, 114
Fitzgerald, F. Scott, 108, 114
Forgione, Louis
    Men of Silence, 29, 67
    Reamer Lou, 62, 67, 73, 74, 78–82, 86
    The River Between, 5, 62, 67–69, 74–75, 80–86
Forman, Henry James, 36–37
The Fortunate Pilgram (Puzo), 24–25, 59
French, passing as, 73
Friedman, Lester D., 30
Full of Life (Fante), 100–101, 119

Gambino, Richard, 22, 29, 59
Gan, Herbert J., 21
Ganick, Peter, 6
Gardaphé, Fred L., 38n1, 50, 53, 59, 68
    Italian Signs, 23
    Leaving Little Italy, 142, 161
    on Sorrentino, 5
Gerber, David, 21–22
Gillan, Maria Mazziotti, 77n7
Gioia, Dana, 110, 156–157
Giunta, Edvige, 165, 166, 167
The Godfather (Puzo), 25
Golden Wedding (Pagano), 122, 125, 126–134
Gordon, Neil, 107–108
Grant, Madison, 28, 31, 33–34

Hallowell, A. Irving, 14
Hamsun, Knut, 63–64
"Heartfelt" (Spiziri), 155
The Heart of the Stranger (McLeod), 29
Hendin, Josephine Gattuso

The Right Thing to Do, 67–68, 76–77, 84–85, 90–91, 169–170, 177
writing on Flannery O'Connor, 166
"History Lessons for Friday" (Papaleo), 143
Hollywood and the Profession of Authorship, 1928-1940 (Fine), 109
Hollywood Italian (Bondanella), 31
How the Other Half Lives (Riis), 28, 44–45
Humor, 100–101, 102
Hunger (Hamsun), 63–64

Identity, 4–7, 69–72, 94–95
Immigrants
  anger of, 67–69, 77–86
  diversity of, 18–23
  trauma of, 70–72, 78
Industrial systems of America, 57
"Inside Bradlee's Department Store" (Barbarese), 162
Isherwood, Christopher, 139–140
The Italian, 28–29, 31–34, 37
Italian American Discussion Group, 23
The Italian Americans (Rolle), 70–71
Italian American women
  gender and immigration experience, 68–69
  power and, 172
  writing tradition, 165–167
  See also Ermelino, Louisa; *specific women writers*
Italian Baptist Missionary Association, 1, 41–42, 43
Italian Signs (Gardaphé), 23
The Italians of New York (Federal Writers' Project), 19
Italian Stories (Papaleo), 144–146

Italy
  automobile culture, 142–143, 147–148
  as destination suburb, 147–151
  as escape/sanctuary, 87–90, 98–99, 102–103, 104–105, 137–138
  returning to, 91–96, 138–142
  as strap for discipline, 87–88, 90–91, 98–99, 101, 104
  as theme park, 142
Izenour, Steven, 158

Jacobson, Matthew Frye, 72–73
Jewish Americans, 21, 39, 47–49
Joey Dee Gets Wise (Ermelino), 164–165, 168–170, 172, 175
The John Fante Reader (Cooper), 106
Juliani, Richard N., 153–154
Jurca, Catherine, 135–136, 141

Kallen, Horace, 37
Kammen, Michael, 18
Kellor, Frances A., 47
Kordich, Catherine J., 107
Krieger, Alex, 141
Kuklick, Bruce, 12

Language acquisition, 60–62
Lankevich, George J., 20
Lape, Esther Everett, 46–47
Lapolla, Garibaldi M., 23
The Last Tycoon (Fitzgerald), 108, 114
Laurino, Maria, 4, 72n3, 94–95
Lawton, Ben, 28
Learning from Las Vegas (Venturi, Brown and Izenour), 158
Leaving Little Italy (Gardaphé), 142, 161
Leopardi, Giacomo, 154
Levi, Carlo, 19, 21

"Light" (D'Angelo), 63
Lindsay, Vachel, 32
Literacy, 48, 49, 59–62
Little Caesar, 37
Littlefield, Walter, 73, 73n4
Little Italies, 142, 156–157, 161

The Madonna of 115th Street (Orsi), 16, 69, 88
"The Mafia and the Movies" (Lawton), 28
Mafia images, 28, 29–30, 34
"Mama Ravioli" (Fante and Wills), 97
Mangano, Antonio, 91
Mangione, Jerre, 24, 47–48, 70, 124–125, 161
  See also *Mount Allegro* (Mangione)
The Man in the Grey Flannel Suit (Wilson), 137, 149
Mannino, Mary Ann, 71
Marcovaldo (Calvino), 140
Mariano, John Horace, 10
Marketplace for literary works, 167
Marshall, Alex, 141
McLeod, Christian, 29
Memory, 154
Mencken, H. L., 96, 109–111
Men of Silence (Forgione), 29, 67
The Milk of Almonds (DeSalvo and Giunta), 166, 167
Miller, Perry, 12
Miss Giardino (Bryant), 67–69, 77–78, 85
Mobsters, 169
Monster (Dunne), 109
Mount Allegro (Mangione), 91–92, 125, 127–128, 161
Mount Vernon distillery example, 9, 16
Mulberry Street, 163
My Dog Stupid (Fante), 87, 102–104, 117–118, 124

Myth-symbol school, 12–13

Naples, Italy, 147–148, 150n3
Narrative categories, 23
Neighborhood rewards/limitations, 168–177
Network of cultures, 15
The New England Mind (Miller), 12
New Historicism, 17–18
New York
  Bensonhurst, 177
  general depictions, 75–76, 78, 86
  Mulberry Street, 163
  Naples comparison, 147–148
  Scarsdale, 145
1933 Was a Bad Year (Fante), 100, 111–112
"The Nordic Type" (Barolini), 93–94

"The Odyssey of a Wop" (Fante), 73
Orsi, Robert
  D'Angelo compared to, 58
  "The Fault of Memory," 87–88, 104
  The Madonna of 115th Street, 16, 56–57, 69, 88, 170, 172
Our Movie Made Children (Forman), 36–37
Out of Place (Papaleo), 88–89, 95–96, 137, 143, 144, 146–151

The Paesanos (Pagano), 122, 123, 125–127, 131, 133
Pagano, Jo
  The Condemned, 122, 123, 126–127
  "The Disinherited," 122–123
  Fante comparison, 122–124
  Golden Wedding, 122, 125, 126–134
  as model for character in *My Dog Stupid*, 124

The Paesanos, 122, 123, 125–127, 131, 133
    Riis comparison, 125–126
Panunzio, Constantine, 67, 71
Papaleo, Joseph
    "Arete," 140–141
    college writings, 136–137
    "History Lessons for Friday," 143
    Italian Stories, 144–146
    life of, 135
    Out of Place, 88–89, 95–96, 137, 143, 144, 146–151
    "The Tony Chapter," 143–144
Paper Fish (De Rosa), 89–90
Parati, Graziella, 150
Parrington, Vernon Louis, 12
The Passing of the Great Race (Grant), 28, 31
Pentecostalism example, 16
Philadelphia. *See* Barbarese, J. T.; Spiziri, Frank S.
Pick-and-shovel man. *See* D'Angelo, Pascal
Poor Little Peppina, 28–29, 31–32, 34–36, 37
Post-ethnic theory, 92–94
Postmodern ethnic optimism, 159
Prosperity, 137–138, 143
"Public School No. 18" (Gillan), 77n7
Puzo, Mario, 24–25, 59, 68

Quinn, Roseanne Giannini, 94n2

"Races" and Americanization, 72–77
Radhakrishnan, R., 69–70
Radical politics, 20–21
"Radio-cinematic brave new world," 136–137
Reamer Lou (Forgione), 62, 67, 73, 74, 78–82, 86
Rebel Without a Cause, 15
Redemption, 169–170

Religion, 16
"Report on 'Grand Central Terminal'" (Szilard), 10–11
The Right Thing to Do (Hendin), 67–68, 76–77, 84–85, 90–91, 169–170
Riis, Jacob, 28, 38–45, 125–126
The River Between (Forgione), 5, 62, 67–69, 74–75, 80–86
The Road to Los Angeles (Fante), 63, 101, 112
Rolle, Andrew, 68, 70–71
Roosevelt, Theodore, 47
Rosenfeld, Isaac, 39, 47, 49
Ruotolo, Lucio, 20–21

Sanctuary. *See* Escape/sanctuary
Saroyan, William, 106
Sayre, Joel, 115
Scarsdale (New York), 145
Screenwriting and literary writing, 107–111
Self
    concept of, 14
    post-ethnic sense of, 93–94
    rejection of, 76–78
Sexuality as threatening, 28–29
A Single Man (Isherwood), 139–140
The Sisters Mallone (Ermelino), 164–165, 168, 172, 174–178
Son of Italy (D'Angelo)
    Bok's work compared to, 38–42
    dedication to Forgione, 73, 73n4
    family depicted in, 58–59, 65
    reviews of, 38, 53–54, 56
    Riis's work compared to, 38–45
    significance of, 49, 51
    struggles depicted in, 56–57, 63–66
    summary of, 54–56
Sorrentino, Gilbert, 5
Soskin (Fante's editor), 118–119

Speranza, Gino, 12, 71–72, 71–72n2, 72n3
Spiziri, Frank S., 152, 153–156, 161
The Split-Level Trap, 139, 143
Spotnitz, Frank, 111
Sprawl, 141–142
Star Trek, 15
Steinberg, Stephen, 20, 48
Stereotypes, 122, 143–144
Suburban life, 135–136, 139–142, 149–150
Szilard, Leo, 10–11

Talese, Gay, 48
Tamburri, Anthony Julian, 63
Their Other Side (Barolini), 138, 139–140
Three Circles of Light (di Donato), 25–26
Tichi, Cecelia, 13
The Time of Your Life (Saroyan), 106
"The Toilers" (D'Angelo), 40–41, 75–76
"The Tony Chapter" (Papaleo), 143–144
Trachtenberg, Alan, 12–13
2001, 14

Umbertina (Barolini), 70, 71, 92–93, 137–138, 156
Under the Blue Moon (Barbarese), 160–161
Unspeakable Images (Friedman), 30

Van Doren, Carl, 40, 50–51, 53
Vecoli, Rudolph J., 22, 98
Venturi, Robert, 157–159
Vertigo (DeSalvo), 163–164, 166

Wait Until Spring, Bandini (Fante), 87, 97, 98–99, 112–113
We, the Divided (Bodei), 142

Were You Always an Italian? (Laurino), 94–95
Wills, Ross B., 87, 97, 106, 118, 120–121
Wilson, Sloan, 137, 149
Wise, Gene, 11–12
Women. *See* Italian American women
Writing with an Accent (Giunta), 165

Yans-McLaughlin, Virginia, 21

About the Author

DENNIS BARONE is Professor of English and Director of the American Studies Program at Saint Joseph College in West Hartford, Conn.

Barone is the author of three books of short fiction: *Abusing the Telephone* (1994), *The Returns* (1996), and *Echoes* (1997), winner of the America Award. He is also the author of two novellas, *Temple of the Rat* (2000) and *God's Whisper* (2005). *Precise Machine*, a hybrid-work of memoir, prose poetry, and short fiction was published by Quale Press in 2006 and a second mixed-genre work, *North Arrow*, in 2008.

He is editor of *Beyond the Red Notebook: Essays on Paul Auster* (University of Pennsylvania Press, 1995), a collection of short prose pieces, *The Walls of Circumstance* (2004), and a selected poems, *Separate Objects* (1998). His essays on American literature and culture have appeared in *American Studies, Critique, Proceedings of the American Philosophical Society, Review of Contemporary Fiction,* and *Voices in Italian Americana*. Barone also gathered the manuscript for and provided a foreword for the Poet's Press edition of John Burnett Payne's posthumous poetry volume, *Walt and Emily/Emily and Walt*.

A graduate of Bard College, he received his Ph.D. in American Civilization from the University of Pennsylvania in 1984, and in 1992 he held the Thomas Jefferson Chair, a distinguished Fulbright lecturing award, in the Netherlands. In 2009 Dennis Barone was named the second West Hartford Poet Laureate in the town's history.

SAGGISTICA

Taking its name from the Italian–which means essays, essay writing, or non fiction–*Saggisitca* is a referred book series dedicated to the study of all topics, individuals, and cultural productions that fall under what we might consider that larger umbrella of all things Italian and Italian/American.

Vito Zagarrio
 The "Un-Happy Ending": Re-viewing The Cinema of Frank Capra. 2011. ISBN 978-1-59954-005-4. Volume 1.

Paolo A. Giordano, editor
 The Hyphenate Writer and The Legacy of Exile. 2010. ISBN 978-1-59954-007-8. Volume 2.

The following volumes are forthcoming:

Fred L. Gardaphè
 The Art of Reading Italian Americana. 2011. ISBN 978-1-59954-019-1. Volume 4.

Anthony Julian Tamburri
 Re-viewing Italian Americana: Generalities and Specificities on Cinema. 2011. ISBN 978-1-59954-020-7. Volume 5.

The following volumes are in preparation:

Sheryl Lynn Postman
 An Italian Writer's Journey through American Realities: Giose Rimanelli's English Novels. "The most tormented decade of America: the 60s" Volume 6.

David Barone and Peter Covino, editors
 Essays on Italian American Literature and Culture. Volume 7.

Peter Carravetta
 After Identity: Critical Challenges in Italian American Poetics and Culture. Volume 8.